GAYLORD

CHIEF JOSEPH

NORTH AMERICAN INDIANS OF ACHIEVEMENT

CHIEF JOSEPH
Nez Perce Leader

ᐯᐯᐯ

Marian W. Taylor

Senior Consulting Editor
W. David Baird
Howard A. White Professor of History
Pepperdine University

CHELSEA HOUSE PUBLISHERS

New York   Philadelphia

FRONTISPIECE   Chief Joseph sat for this portrait by Edward S. Curtis, probably the nation's best-known photographer of American Indians, around 1903.

ON THE COVER   Chief Joseph, also known as Hin-mah-too-yah-lat-kekht (Thunder-rolling-in-the-mountains), spent most of his life battling for the rights of his people, the Nez Perce Indians.

Chelsea House Publishers

EDITORIAL DIRECTOR   Richard Scott Rennert
EXECUTIVE EDITOR   Sean Dolan
EXECUTIVE MANAGING EDITOR   Karyn Gullen Browne
COPY CHIEF   Philip Koslow
PICTURE EDITOR   Adrian G. Allen
ART DIRECTOR   Nora Wertz
MANUFACTURING DIRECTOR   Gerald Levine
SYSTEMS MANAGER   Lindsey Ottman
PRODUCTION COORDINATOR   Marie Claire Cebrián-Ume

North American Indians of Achievement

SENIOR EDITOR   Sean Dolan

Staff for CHIEF JOSEPH

EDITORIAL ASSISTANT   Nicole Greenblatt
SENIOR DESIGNER   Rae Grant
PICTURE RESEARCHER   Alan Gottlieb
COVER ILLUSTRATOR   Janet Hamlin

First Printing

1   3   5   7   9   8   6   4   2

Library of Congress Cataloging-in-Publication Data

Taylor, Marian W.
Chief Joseph, Nez Perce Leader/Marian W. Taylor
    p. cm.—(North American Indians of achievement)
Includes bibliographical references and index.
Summary: Presents the life and times of the Nez Perce Indian chief who led his people on a great trek to escape the injustices of the American government.
ISBN 0-7910-1708-7
ISBN 0-7910-1972-1 (pbk.)
1. Joseph, Nez Perce Chief, 1840–1904—Juvenile literature. 2. Nez Perce Indians—Biography—Juvenile literature. 3. Nez Perce Indians—Kings and Rulers—Biography. [1. Joseph, Nez Perce Chief, 1840–1904. 2. Nez Perce Indians—Biography. 3. Indians of North America—Biography.] I. Title. II. Series.
E99.N5J677 1993   92-31311
979'.004974—dc20   CIP
    [B]   AC

CONTENTS

NORTH AMERICAN INDIANS OF ACHIEVEMENT

BLACK HAWK
Sac Rebel

JOSEPH BRANT
Mohawk Chief

COCHISE
Apache Chief

CRAZY HORSE
Sioux War Chief

CHIEF GALL
Sioux War Chief

GERONIMO
Apache Warrior

HIAWATHA
Founder of the Iroquois
Confederacy

CHIEF JOSEPH
Nez Perce Leader

PETER MACDONALD
Former Chairman of the Navajo
Nation

WILMA MANKILLER
Principal Chief of the Cherokees

OSCEOLO
Seminole Rebel

QUANAH PARKER
Comanche Chief

KING PHILIP
Wampanoag Rebel

POCAHONTAS
Powhatan Peacemaker

PONTIAC
Ottawa Rebel

RED CLOUD
Sioux War Chief

WILL ROGERS
Cherokee Entertainer

SEQUOYAH
Inventor of the Cherokee Alphabet

SITTING BULL
Chief of the Sioux

TECUMSEH
Shawnee Rebel

JIM THORPE
Sac and Fox Athlete

SARAH WINNEMUCCA
Northern Paiute Writer and
Diplomat

Other titles in preparation

ON INDIAN LEADERSHIP

by W. David Baird
Howard A. White Professor of History
Pepperdine University

Authoritative utterance is in thy mouth, perception is in thy heart, and thy tongue is the shrine of justice," the ancient Egyptians said of their king. From him, the Egyptians expected authority, discretion, and just behavior. Homer's *Iliad* suggests that the Greeks demanded somewhat different qualities from their leaders: justice and judgment, wisdom and counsel, shrewdness and cunning, valor and action. It is not surprising that different people living at different times should seek different qualities from the individuals they looked to for guidance. By and large, a people's requirements for leadership are determined by two factors: their culture and the unique circumstances of the time and place in which they live.

Before the late 15th century, when non-Indians first journeyed to what is now North America, most Indian tribes were not ruled by a single person. Instead, there were village chiefs, clan headmen, peace chiefs, war chiefs, and a host of other types of leaders, each with his or her own specific duties. These influential people not only decided political matters but also helped shape their tribe's social, cultural, and religious life. Usually, Indian leaders held their positions because they had won the respect of their peers. Indeed, if a leader's followers at any time decided that he or she was out of step with the will of the people, they felt free to look to someone else for advice and direction.

Thus, the greatest achievers in traditional Indian communities were men and women of extraordinary talent. They were not only skilled at navigating the deadly waters of tribal politics and cultural customs but also able to, directly or indirectly, make a positive and significant difference in the daily life of their followers.

From the beginning of their interaction with Native Americans, non-Indians failed to understand these features of Indian leadership. Early European explorers and settlers merely assumed that Indians had the same relationship with their leaders as non-Indians had with their kings and queens. European monarchs generally inherited their positions and ruled large nations however they chose, often with little regard for the desires or needs of their subjects. As a result, the settlers of Jamestown saw Pocahontas as a "princess" and Pilgrims dubbed Wampanoag leader Metacom "King Philip," envisioning them in roles very different from those in which their own people placed them.

As more and more non-Indians flocked to North America, the nature of Indian leadership gradually began to change. Influential Indians no longer had to take on the often considerable burden of pleasing only their own people; they also had to develop a strategy of dealing with the non-Indian newcomers. In a rapidly changing world, new types of Indian role models with new ideas and talents continually emerged. Some were warriors; others were peacemakers. Some held political positions within their tribes; others were writers, artists, religious prophets, or athletes. Although the demands of Indian leadership altered from generation to generation, several factors that determined which Indian people became prominent in the centuries after first contact remained the same.

Certain personal characteristics distinguished these Indians of achievement. They were intelligent, imaginative, practical, daring, shrewd, uncompromising, ruthless, and logical. They were constant in friendships, unrelenting in hatreds, affectionate with their relatives, and respectful to their God or gods. Of course, no single Native American leader embodied all these qualities, nor these qualities only. But it was these characteristics that allowed them to succeed.

The special skills and talents that certain Indians possessed also brought them to positions of importance. The life of Hiawatha, the legendary founder of the powerful Iroquois Confederacy, displays the value that oratorical ability had for many Indians in power.

The biography of Cochise, the 19th-century Apache chief, illustrates that leadership often required keen diplomatic skills not only in transactions among tribespeople but also in hardheaded negotiations with non-Indians. For others, such as Mohawk Joseph Brant and Navajo Peter MacDonald, a non-Indian education proved advantageous in their dealings with other peoples.

Sudden changes in circumstance were another crucial factor in determining who became influential in Indian communities. King Philip in the 1670s and Geronimo in the 1880s both came to power when their people were searching for someone to lead them into battle against white frontiersmen who had forced upon them a long series of indignities. Seeing the rising discontent of Indians of many tribes in the 1810s, Tecumseh and his brother, the Shawnee prophet Tenskwatawa, proclaimed a message of cultural revitalization that appealed to thousands. Other Indian achievers recognized cooperation with non-Indians as the most advantageous path during their lifetime. Sarah Winnemucca in the late 19th century bridged the gap of understanding between her people and their non-Indian neighbors through the publication of her autobiography *Life Among the Piutes*. Olympian Jim Thorpe in the early 20th century championed the assimilationist policies of the U.S. government and, with his own successes, demonstrated the accomplishments Indians could make in the non-Indian world. And Wilma Mankiller, principal chief of the Cherokees, continues to fight successfully for the rights of her people through the courts and through negotiation with federal officials.

Leadership among Native Americans, just as among all other peoples, can be understood only in the context of culture and history. But the centuries that Indians have had to cope with invasions of foreigners in their homelands have brought unique hardships and obstacles to the Native American individuals who most influenced and inspired others. Despite these challenges, there has never been a lack of Indian men and women equal to these tasks. With such strong leaders, it is no wonder that Native Americans remain such a vital part of this nation's cultural landscape.

Twenty-five hundred strong, a band of Nez Perce Indians thunders into the Walla Walla Valley council grounds on May 24, 1855. Greeting the Indians—who include Old Joseph and his 15-year-old son, Young Joseph—are Washington Territory officials, including Governor Isaac Stevens (mounted, at right of flagpole).

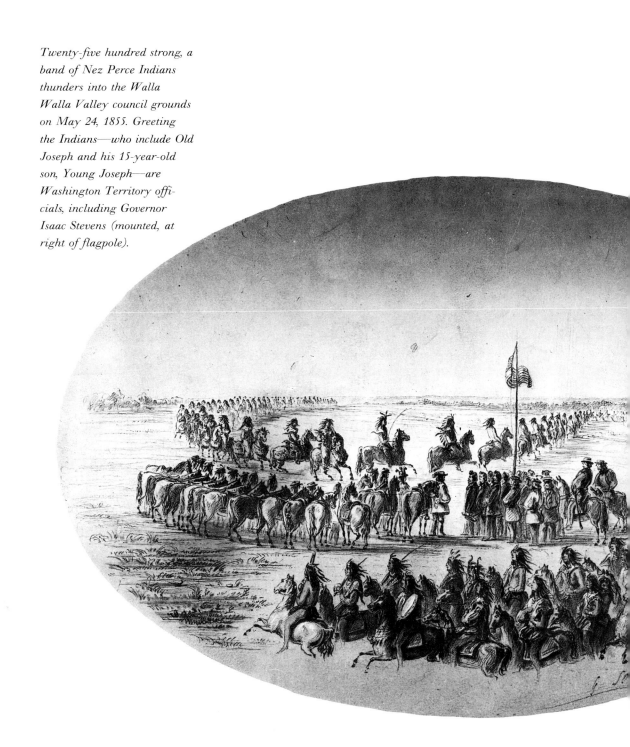

1

JOSEPH'S WORLD

Into the valley they came, riding hard in the noonday sun. Stretching as far as the eye could see, the column of 2,500 Indians and horses thundered toward the American flag waving over Mill Creek in Washington Territory. The sun, dazzling on this hot day—May 24, 1855—glinted off the riders' painted faces, feather headdresses, flamboyantly decorated horses, and flashing knives, guns, shields, and lances.

The Indians galloped straight for the flagpole and the white men clustered around it. Suddenly, 1,000 warriors separated themselves from the others. Reining up, they formed a long line across the plain and waited in motionless silence. Then, with a roar, they charged forward again, splitting the air with a barrage of drumbeats, clashing shields, and bone-rattling shrieks.

The warriors, reported one of the onlookers later, approached "at a gallop, two abreast, naked to the breechclout, their faces covered with white, red, and yellow paint." Both men and mounts were "arrayed in the most glaring finery. They were painted with such colors as formed the greatest contrast; the white being smeared with crimson in fantastic figures, and the dark colors streaked with white clay."

The Indians—members of the Wallowa Valley Nez Perce tribe—made a fearsome spectacle, but they had come in friendship. They planned to meet the white men at a council, and had dressed and acted fiercely to show themselves as a powerful people. Also invited to this council in the Walla Walla Valley were a number of other regional tribes: Yakimas, Cayuses, Walla Wallas, and Umatillas. The Nez Perces intended to stand out from the others.

Meeting the Indians was a group of federal and territorial officials led by Isaac Ingalls Stevens, governor and superintendent of Indian affairs for Washington Territory. Stevens, who had supervised a survey of the territory for the Pacific Railroad, wanted to clear a northern route for the line and to open up the area for

Lawyer, the Nez Perce crier designated by Governor Stevens as his people's spokesman, wears his trademark outfit in this sketch from the 1850s. His apparel, a mix of Indian and white styles, includes a tall silk hat embellished with hawk feathers.

white settlement. An energetic, ambitious West Point graduate, the 37-year-old Massachusetts-born governor dreamed of building a Pacific Northwest empire of white settlers. To reach his goals, he needed land. He had invited the Indians to this meeting to get it; he was determined to obtain their chiefs' signatures on a treaty that would cede much of their territory to the U.S. government.

The Nez Perces were represented by several tribal chiefs, including Big Thunder (also known as James), Lawyer (a name that started out as Aleiya), Red Wolf, and Joseph. The latter, usually called Old Joseph, had brought along his son, a 15-year-old known as Young Joseph. The young man took no direct part in the conferences, but his father probably talked to him each evening about the day's events.

Old Joseph and the other chiefs had little enthusiasm for Stevens's treaty. Still, they were not deeply worried about it, believing that the whites would not enforce it for many years. Furthermore, they wanted to keep peace with these Americans. The Nez Perces had a long history of friendly relations with whites, and they were proud of it. Members of the tribe often boasted, in fact, that no Nez Perce had ever killed a white man.

After the opening formalities, the council got down to business. Stevens told the Indians that the United States wanted them to sign treaties limiting their freedom and placing them under government control. After selling most of their land to the government, they would settle on reservations with carefully defined boundaries.

The government, he said, planned to create three reservations: one for the Nez Perces, one for the Yakimas, and a third for the Umatillas, Walla Wallas, and Cayuses. Under the agreements, some of the Indians would be able to keep part of their former domains, but they would still

be governed by agents of the U.S. Bureau of Indian Affairs (BIA).

In return for the Indians' move, Stevens and his colleagues explained, the Indians would receive cash plus federal supervision. The government pledged to build schools, sawmills, and shops and to train the Indians to farm and work with machinery. They could become "civilized" human beings, assimilate themselves into white culture, and thus greatly improve their lives.

The Nez Perces and others, the officials added, might one day even have children who would grow up to be doctors, lawyers, and other professionals. Although they never mentioned Christianity directly, the whites implied that the Native Americans would benefit by embracing it. To the Indians, all this was strange talk indeed. Why should they want to imitate white "civilization"?

Like most Native Americans, Young Joseph had been taught reverence for the land, regarded by the Indians as the mother of all mankind. The thought of their land being bought and sold probably disturbed him as much as it did the adults at the council. Stevens's proposals, in fact, pleased almost none of the Indians. Chief Peopeo Moxmox (Yellow Bird) of the Walla Wallas, the first to respond to the deal, delivered a barbed speech in which he told the whites he did not "see the offer you have made to the Indians." He wondered aloud why any Indian would agree to surrender his lands to live under the thumb of the white man.

Then Young Chief of the Cayuses made a long and eloquent speech, pointing out that the Great Spirit had only entrusted the Indians with the land's care, and that they had no right to sell it. "I wonder if the ground is listening to what is said," he mused. "I wonder if the ground has anything to say." Chief Owhi of the Yakimas reminded the group that the Great Spirit had "named our lands for us to take care of."

The Indians' tribal system involved many small bands, each living in its own village and each following its own set of leaders. The head chief counseled and advised the band; its members accepted his advice or not, as they chose. Assisting the head chief were medicine men and

minor chiefs, or headmen. Each band also had a war chief; he was under the head chief except in times of conflict, when he became the band's top leader. The system puzzled Stevens and other whites. To their way of thinking, each tribe should have a paramount chief who ruled over all the separate bands; it was only with such a leader that the whites wished to deal. If a tribe could present no "supreme chief," Stevens often appointed one himself.

To the Indians Lawyer was probably no more than a camp crier, a person who transmitted news from one village to the other, but at the Walla Walla council, Stevens decided to treat him as head chief of all the Nez Perces. The Indians did not understand this position, but they made no argument about Lawyer's selection—an acceptance that would one day lead to tragedy—and Lawyer wound up doing most of their negotiating. Under the treaty he worked out with Stevens, the Nez Perces would give up part of their territory, but they would be guaranteed the right to hunt and fish on that land "forever." They would live on a reservation carved out of their traditional homeland. There, the government

Standing under a willow-sapling tent, Stevens (center, wearing light-colored trousers) addresses Indians at Walla Walla. Speech making was slow work: after each sentence, the governor had to stop and wait while interpreters translated his words into the languages of the Nez Perces, Cayuses, Walla Wallas, and Umatillas.

would pay the chiefs small annual allowances and would provide schools, training, livestock, and tools for the people.

None of the Nez Perces liked the treaty much, but the chiefs understood their options: accept the deal or lose their land and get nothing at all. On June 11, 1855, after being assured that the Wallowa Valley—heart of the Nez Perce homeland—would be part of their reservation, Old Joseph signed the treaty, the third chief to do so. Neither Young Joseph nor his father could know it at the time, but that signature would change the lives of the Nez Perces forever.

Joseph Taawé-tak-hes. *suiawnan*
Cchief of the Nez perré Indians

2

LAND OF THE
WINDING WATERS

The man known to history as Chief Joseph was born in 1840 near what is now the Oregon-Washington border. His birthplace was in the Wallowa Valley—Land of the Winding Waters—where countless generations of his ancestors had lived and died.

Young Joseph and his family were members of the Wallowa band of the Nez Perce tribe. French trappers, observing around 1750 that some of these Indians wore seashells in their noses as decorations, called them Nez Percé (pierced nose). The tribespeople had called themselves Numípu (roughly, "we people"), but they liked the Frenchmen's name, which they pronounced *nez purse*, and they adopted it permanently.

Young Joseph, who made his first appearance in a cave near Joseph Creek, was the firstborn child of Khap-khap-on-imi and Tu-eka-kas, a chief of the Nez Perce Wallowa band. The youngster's birth was followed by those of numerous brothers and sisters. Of these, Ollokot (Frog) became Young Joseph's inseparable companion. Although the boys were at least a year apart in age, they always looked so much alike that most people—especially whites—would later assume they were twins.

Few facts about Young Joseph's early life are known, but he and Ollokot must have grown up like most boys of their tribe, rambling about their village—naked when they were toddlers—with the other boys, watching as the

This portrait of Old Joseph (father of the future Chief Joseph), was sketched by Private Gustavus Sohon, Governor Stevens's military aide, in 1855. Originally called Tu-eka-kas, Old Joseph received his new name from Christian missionary Henry Spalding in 1839.

women ground roots for flour, spread berries on mats to dry in the sun, and scraped hides with sharp stones. They would have seen young warriors plucking feathers from captive eagles to decorate their war bonnets and listened to the elders tell stories of their people.

Young Joseph and his brother would have heard tales of the strangers who came to their land many years earlier, the white explorers who had stayed with the Nez Perces for a while. One autumn, these men had left their horses and gear with the Indians and traveled further west by river. They returned in the spring, found all their possessions safe with their Nez Perce friends, and exchanged gifts with them before heading back east. (The explorers were Meriwether Lewis and William Clark, sent

A Nez Perce man, painted by Canadian artist Paul Kane in 1847, wears the shell nose ornament that prompted French trappers to give the tribe its name, French for "pierced nose," in the mid-18th century.

Presented to the Nez Perces by Meriwether Lewis and William Clark, a medallion calls for "Peace and Friendship" between the U.S. government and Native Americans. President Thomas Jefferson sent explorers Lewis and Clark to visit the Nez Perces and other Far West Indian tribes in the early 1800s.

in 1804 by President Thomas Jefferson to chart the Far West.)

The tribe's old men and women would also have told the children folk stories and myths, including the legend about the creation of the Nez Perce people. Nez Perce history, said the elders, began when a huge sea monster came ashore and began roaming the Kamiah Valley (in what is now northern Idaho). Endlessly hungry, the creature began eating all the animals in the country. When Coyote (the perennial prankster and rascal of Indian lore) heard about the monster, he decided to test his wits against the creature's strength. The monster ate Coyote, too, but Coyote had not lost yet. He had a knife hidden in his belt, and once inside the monster, he cut out his heart and killed him.

Fox had been watching the battle. When Coyote emerged from the dead beast, Fox suggested that the two of them cut up the body and make people. Coyote liked the idea. From the monster's head, they made the Flathead tribe; from its feet, the Blackfoot Indians; from each of the other parts, another Indian nation. After a while, nothing remained but the heart, which Coyote held up. Drops of the heart's blood fell on the ground, and from them sprang a new race of people, proud, tall, strong, and wise—the Nez Perce. The Great Spirit was pleased by this, so he turned the heart into an enormous stone, which can still be seen in the Kamiah Valley.

When Young Joseph was five years old, his parents took him to the Protestant mission at Lapwai (the place of the butterfly), a village at the junction of Lapwai Creek and the Clearwater River. Here, Protestant missionaries Henry Harmon Spalding and his wife, Eliza, had been teaching English and giving Bible lessons since 1836. In 1839, the year before Young Joseph's birth, Tu-eka-kas had accepted Christianity, been baptized Joseph, and been formally married to his wife by Spalding. Receptive and open-minded, Old Joseph had realized that these strangers could teach his people useful skills, and he urged other members of his band to learn the "white man's Book," or Bible.

Spalding also baptized five-year-old Young Joseph and enrolled him and Ollokot in the mission's Sunday school. The boys happily attended classes while their parents took part in Spalding's services, but all this came to an end with violence. The trouble began in Cayuse territory, some 120 miles south of Lapwai, where Spalding's colleague, missionary-doctor Marcus Whitman, had opened a mission.

When an epidemic of measles broke out among the Cayuses, some of them believed Whitman had practiced "bad magic" on them, and in 1847, a band of warriors massacred him and 14 other whites. Soon afterward, a group of young Nez Perce warriors looted Spalding's house, an act that chilled the relationship between the clergyman and Old Joseph. The Nez Perce chief dropped the white man's religion and led his family away from the mission, thus ending the formal education of Young Joseph and his brother.

A visitor studies the Heart of the Monster in Idaho's Kamiah Valley. According to Nez Perce legend, the enormous stone appeared after Coyote killed an evil sea monster and he and Fox changed its heart's blood into the mighty Nez Perce tribe. Pleased with the new people, the Great Spirit marked the site forever by turning the heart to stone.

Missionary Henry Harmon Spalding arrived in the upper Midwest in 1836, determined to substitute his own brand of stern Christianity for the "savage" religion of the natives. He made some converts—including Old Joseph—but his harsh ways turned many Indians away from him and his message: eight years after Spalding baptized him, Old Joseph returned to his native faith.

Old Joseph, however, continued the boy's education in spiritual matters. As an adult, Young Joseph spoke about his childhood training:

> Our fathers gave us many laws, which they had learned from their fathers. These laws . . . told us to treat all men as they treated us; that we should never be the first to break a bargain; that it was a disgrace to tell a lie; that we should speak only the truth. . . . We were taught to believe that the Great Spirit sees and hears everything, and that he never forgets; that hereafter he will give everyman a spirit home according to his deserts. . . . This I believe, and all my people believe the same.

Old Joseph's teachings may have been influenced by the Christianity he had renounced, but basically, he taught his boys the same lessons Nez Perce fathers had been teaching their children for hundreds of years. During all those centuries, the Nez Perces had roamed the region where the present-day states of Oregon, Washington, and Idaho meet. They lived by hunting deer, elk, and antelope, and by catching the region's huge salmon and other fish. In the summers, the tribe's women and children gathered winter food—roots, wild onions, and berries—while the men crossed the Bitterroot Mountains to stalk buffalo in what is now Montana. The Nez Perces also raised sleek horses and fat cattle.

Other whites had followed the 18th-century French trappers, but the Nez Perces remained peaceful, welcoming and often helping the traders and explorers who entered their territory. The Nez Perces' name for the whites—Big Hearts of the East—indicates their sentiments toward them.

But as Young Joseph grew up, the winds of change were blowing hard. Native Americans of the Northwest faced not only missionaries intent on destroying the Indians' old ways but also a rising wave of non-Indian immigration. With the newcomers came an assortment of new conditions, none of them good for the Indians.

The immigrants brought smallpox, measles, influenza, and other contagious diseases to which the Indians had no immunity. By the untold thousands, Indians died from these plagues.

And the non-Indians who poured into the West wanted land, Indian land, for their crops and livestock. Whenever it appeared difficult to acquire, the settlers complained about the "Indian problem"—a troublesome business they hoped the federal government would soon eliminate. White Americans moved onto lands in western Oregon that had belonged to the Clatsops, Tillamooks, Siletzes, Clowwewallas, Atfalatis, and others.

Even as late as Young Joseph's 10th year, however, few whites had entered the inland Northwest, an area commonly called the Columbia Plateau. Still, the plateau Indians—who included Joseph's band of Nez Perces—suspected that it was only a matter of time until whites decided to settle on their territory. As a child, Young Joseph may have considered the problem of white expansion, but it is unlikely. He was probably, like boys everywhere, more interested in action, in running, riding, climbing trees, and racing through the woods with his friends.

Joseph spent most of his youth traveling with his family on its seasonal rounds. In the late winter of each year, the people of his band dismantled their tipis (conical tents constructed of poles and buffalo hides), rounded up their horses, loaded their household goods onto travoises (platforms attached to a pair of poles and dragged by humans or horses), and moved out to gather roots on the prairies. The children enjoyed these expeditions, which gave them the chance to visit with youngsters from other Nez Perce bands.

The Nez Perces remained at the root grounds until spring, when the salmon—sockeye, king, and silver—began to run up the Columbia and Snake rivers. Then the tribe's women, including Joseph's mother, once again dismantled the tipis and loaded the horses, this time in preparation for the journey to the fishing areas.

As a boy, Joseph undoubtedly helped his family fish for salmon. He and his brothers and sisters would have gutted the great fish and set them on wood racks to dry in the sun. In September, when the fishing season ended, the Nez Perce men prepared for the fall hunt of deer, elk, bear, and bighorn sheep. The women gathered berries and everyone helped to harvest food to last the family through the winter.

For the Nez Perces, gathering, hunting, and fishing were more than acts of survival; they were spiritual practices. Early in life, young people learned their tribe's religious precepts. When the Indians gathered food, they gave thanks to the Creator through the ceremonies of the First Root and the First Berry. The Nez Perces also held First Salmon ceremonies in which they thanked the salmon for giving its life so that the people might live, and thanked the Creator for providing for them. These ceremonies were major events in the year. At an early age, then, Joseph would have learned a deep and abiding reverence for the earth and its plants and animals.

In the autumn, the Nez Perce parents, grandparents, aunts, and uncles prepared the tribe's youngsters for their vision quest, a ritual in which they would seek their true name and their own *wayakin*, or spirit helper. When the boys and girls were about 10 years old, each went alone and unarmed to a remote area, usually one that held special family significance. The children knew they were to eat and drink nothing, but to wait—for several solitary nights, if necessary—until the spirit revealed itself, perhaps in a dream.

Joseph left no written account of his vision quest, but his nephew, Yellow Wolf, did write about his. In his autobiography, *Yellow Wolf: His Own Story*, he wrote:

A Nez Perce woman (far left) carries kindling into her tipi. Sapling frames covered with buffalo hides, these conical structures sheltered Young Joseph's people during the summer months; in cold weather, the Nez Perces lived in multifamily longhouses.

"Nobody around, just myself. No weapons, for nothing would hurt me. No children ever get hurt when out on such business." It was during Young Joseph's quest that he learned his name: Hin-mah-too-yah-lat-kekht, which means "Thunder-rolling-in-the-mountains."

Each spring, many Nez Perces left their home country to hunt buffalo in Wyoming and Montana. When they had brought down as many of the huge animals as they needed, they cut up the meat and dried it in the sun for future use. Like other Indian buffalo hunters, the Nez Perces used every part of the animal. They tanned the hides for clothing, blankets, and tipis, and they cleaned and sharpened the bones for weapons and tools.

It is likely that as a child, Young Joseph traveled to the buffalo plains to hunt with his family. Both Joseph and Ollokot learned through experience, particularly by working alongside their elders. They accompanied their parents everywhere, even to such significant gatherings as the one held in the Walla Walla Valley in 1855.

After the Walla Walla council, Old Joseph took his family home to live in peace, but peace proved elusive. Not long after his return, Old Joseph learned that whites had discovered gold in Yakima territory, north of the Spokane River. The find quickly attracted crowds of miners, who just as quickly earned the enmity of the Yakimas. Reports began to come in of whites stealing the Indians' horses, raping their women, and killing their men. Yakima warriors speedily retaliated.

In the summer of 1855, when two Yakima men killed an Indian agent, the United States Army stepped in, and the Plateau Indian War began. Old Joseph and his family maintained their friendship with the whites and stayed out of the conflict, which lasted until 1858, but they watched and worried.

In 1859, the U.S. Senate finally ratified the Nez Perce Treaty, which Joseph and his colleagues had signed four years earlier. For another year, relations between the Nez Perces and the whites remained stable. Then came a discovery that signaled the start of a new—and eventually disastrous—chapter in the Nez Perce story.

3

"THEY WERE LIKE THE GRIZZLY BEARS"

Regarded as handsome even in his later years, Joseph was approaching 60 when this portrait was made. No pictures of him before the age of 37 survive, but contemporary accounts suggest that women found him very attractive, not only for his appearance but for his strength, horsemanship, and dignity.

In August 1860, white prospectors discovered gold in the Bitterroot Mountains, part of the land that the 1855 Walla Walla Treaty guaranteed to the Nez Perces "forever." Like all such discoverers, these prospectors tried to keep their find a secret; like all such secrets, it escaped at once. From all across the Northwest, gold-hungry men made a mad dash for Idaho. By the fall of 1861, more than 6,000 prospectors had converged on Nez Perce land. Close on their heels came the parade of traditional hangers-on: prostitutes, merchants, whiskey peddlers, gunmen, and gamblers.

Until news of the miners' invasion reached them in late 1861, Chief Joseph and his band had been enjoying a peaceful year. Believing that the Walla Walla Treaty would protect their lands, the Indians felt secure. They had been blessed with good salmon fishing and a fine buffalo hunt. Many had known personal success as well. In 1860, Young Joseph had visited the Lapwai community. Six feet tall, handsome, powerful, and 20 years old, he was not only a splendid horseman but, according to contemporary accounts, gentle and dignified as well. Not surprisingly, then, when he fell in love with Ta-ma-al-we-non-my, daughter of one of Big Thunder's subchiefs, the beautiful teenager returned his love. Her father and Joseph's approved of the match, and the young couple

married after a round of joyful feasts. The union appears to have been a happy one, although some said Ta-ma-al-we-non-my talked a bit too much. Joseph may have agreed: "When you can get the last word with an echo," he once joked, "you may have the last word with your wife."

That summer, Old Joseph's Nez Perces and their neighbors learned that prospectors had entered the Nez Perce Reservation at Clearwater Canyon, only about 60 miles northeast of the Wallowa Valley. That area's Indians had welcomed the interlopers, seeing them as trading partners from whom they could obtain tools, woolen clothing, and beads in exchange for horses and food. Although the Indians bitterly resented newcomers who intended to settle down and farm, most believed that miners would simply dig for a little while, then move on. Old Joseph's view, however, was less optimistic. Nothing good, he believed, would come of the prospectors' presence.

The newly appointed Nez Perce Indian agent, A. J. Cain, was also skeptical. It was his job to enforce the

Abandoned after the gold rush of the 1860s, the former boom-town of Florence, Idaho, slowly crumbles into ruin. Such communities, which attracted gamblers, gunmen, and saloon keepers, severely disrupted the lives of the Indians whose territory they occupied.

Walla Walla Treaty, which barred nonauthorized whites from the reservation. Besides, he had dealt with miners before. He knew they rarely showed the slightest respect for Indian land, Indian rights, or Indian lives—especially if Indians stood between them and gold. Speaking from his own experience, Cain wrote, "I could fill page after page in portraying the number and nature of the outrages the Indians and their families were subjected to [by miners]."

Cain asked for U.S. troops to clear the area of miners, but the local military commander refused to supply them. The treaty forbade permanent settlers, the officer asserted, but not missionaries, trappers, or miners passing through. He would try to keep them moving, but the Civil War was raging back east, and troops were in short supply. Cain tried to run the miners off himself, but with no success. B. F. Kendall, superintendent of Indian affairs for Washington Territory, understood Cain's problem. "To attempt to restrain miners," he said, "would be, to my mind, like attempting to restrain the whirlwind."

The prospectors kept pouring in. By the spring of 1862, an estimated 30,000 non-Indians had entered Nez Perce Territory; by 1863, they had carried off gold worth many millions of dollars. A few Nez Perces made money by mining or supplying the prospectors' camps, but for the majority, the gold rush was a disaster. Causing the most harm were the whiskey sellers. Young Indians who had never before encountered alcohol and who had no genetic tolerance for it fell easily—and with disastrous consequence—under its powerful influence.

The situation grew worse rapidly. Greed, envy, and racial friction produced crime. Robberies, rapes, and murders—committed by people of both races—escalated; each violent act seemed to inspire two to avenge it. Both whites and Indians realized that unless someone took action quickly, war would sweep the Northwest.

To the Indians, the solution seemed clear: to get these hordes of non-Indians off Indian land, the federal government must enforce the 1855 treaty. To the whites—who, of course, had a much better chance of getting what they wanted from the government—the solution was even simpler: shrink the reservation. That way, the miners would not be trespassing on Indian land and the two ethnic groups would be clearly separated. If the Indians were congregated in a much smaller area—say, 10 percent of the original reservation—added the whites, the army could more easily protect them.

In the spring of 1862, representatives from Washington Territory asked Congress to finance a new treaty council with the Nez Perces. Congress, which needed western gold to finance the bloody and expensive Civil War, wanted a fast settlement of the dispute. The legislators quickly appropriated $50,000 for the council, which was scheduled for May 1863 at Fort Lapwai.

When Old Joseph, at this point about 78 years old, received his invitation to the council, he was dumbfounded. Was it possible that the government planned to break its word, changing the treaty signed only eight years earlier? Yes, said the U.S. Army general who delivered the invitation, but Chief Joseph would soon understand that the new arrangement was highly beneficial to the Nez Perces. Not so, said Joseph. He would attend no new council. He and his fellow chiefs had pledged their faith, the government had pledged its faith, and that was that. No further meetings were needed.

But the new Washington Territory superintendent of Indian affairs, Calvin H. Hale, did schedule a council. Before it took place, a government messenger called on Old Joseph to tell him that Hale had surveyed the boundaries of the proposed new reservation. It was to be a small rectangle of land, just under 800,000 acres, carved

Serene and beautiful, Wallowa Lake lies at the heart of Oregon's Nez Perce country. Although the prospectors who flooded the region in the 1860s disturbed few Nez Perces at first, some observers recognized them as a serious threat: as one experienced official noted, miners were no easier to control than "the whirlwind."

out of the original reservation of 7.7 *million* acres, and it did not include the Wallowa Valley, Old Joseph's beloved homeland. Hale had explained that each Nez Perce family would be alloted a 20-acre plot and allowed to pasture livestock on nearby hillsides. Chief Lawyer, the messenger told Old Joseph, was protesting the new plan vigorously.

Not surprisingly, Old Joseph was appalled; confirming his worst fears, the government was planning to nullify the 1855 treaty. Realizing that a united front was the tribe's only hope, the Nez Perce leader decided his sons Young Joseph and Ollokot would represent him at the council. Before they left, he spoke to 23-year-old Young Joseph in a solemn tone. Years later, Joseph recalled his father's words: "When you go into council with the white man, always remember your country. Do not give it away. The white man will cheat you out of your home."

By the time Young Joseph, Ollokot, and their delegation arrived at Fort Lapwai, some 2,000 Nez Perces had assembled. Discussions began at once. First, Hale and his fellow commissioners confirmed what everyone already knew: that the government proposed to shrink the Nez Perce reservation to a sliver of its then-current size. Then Lawyer rose to speak. The Indians, he said, considered American law "sacred"; because the treaty was part of American law, it too was sacred and could not be violated. Anyone who claimed otherwise, added Lawyer, must be a liar. Hale responded by saying that President Abraham Lincoln was no liar; that he, Lincoln, favored the new treaty as the best way to protect his red children, the Nez Perces.

In a spirit of compromise, the Indian spokesmen offered to sell the land on which the whites had built ferries and towns, and to let the miners continue to dig for gold. This, they said, would not affect the sacred 1855 treaty. Despite this, one chief told Hale, "We cannot give you the country; we cannot sell it to you."

Arguments flew back and forth, with neither side ready to back down. By the end of the day, Hale was sputtering ineffectively; clearly, no remarks of his could persuade the Indians that the government's reneging on its own treaty was a good idea. But this bothered him not at all. He later referred to the Nez Perces' arguments as "buncombe"—baloney.

Getting nowhere in open meetings, Hale arranged to meet some of the more "friendly" Nez Perce chiefs in private. One by one, he promised them rewards for agreeing to the new reservation boundaries. One by one, they caved in, some swayed by the promise of elegant new houses, others seduced by the assurances of government-built schools and other improvements. To Lawyer, Hale painted a rosy picture: on the new, compact reservation, Lawyer would be top man; the antitreaty chiefs would have to grant him the authority and prestige he had earned by arranging the new treaty. Furthermore, said Hale, Lawyer could take credit for all the new buildings and services the government planned to supply to the Indians.

When Young Joseph, Big Thunder, and the other leaders who opposed the new treaty realized how things were going, they called a meeting with Lawyer and his supporters. Fearing violence, Hale sent an observer to the meeting, but it ended peacefully. The opponents agreed to remain "treaty" and "nontreaty" Indians, and to go their separate ways. Lawyer would no longer be their head chief, but the two sides would remain friends. At that, the factions shook hands and parted, prompting Hale's observer to write that he had been present at "the extinguishment of the last council fires of the most powerful Indian nation on the sunset side of the Rocky Mountains."

Young Joseph believed that he and his band had made their point. They would not sell off their territory, no matter what Lawyer and his group did. Seeing no reason to continue talking, Joseph led his people home. Lawyer, meanwhile, rounded up enough other chiefs (all of whom already lived within the boundaries of the proposed new reservation) to make an impressive list of *X*'s on the treaty. On June 9, 52 Indians signed the Nez Perce Treaty of 1863, an agreement that became known to the nontreaty Nez Perces as the Thief Treaty. As Hale saw it, the government had just bought 6,932,270 acres of Nez Perce land for less than 8 cents per acre.

Soon after Congress approved and President Lincoln signed the Treaty of 1863, Old Joseph and the other nontreaty chiefs learned that they were expected to move. Joseph and his band—some 250 people—were to relocate

Indian leaders and U.S. government officials meet to negotiate the 1863 document that would be scornfully known as the Thief Treaty. Accepted by the whites as spokesman for the Nez Perces, Lawyer (seated, center) began by defending his people's land but eventually signed over all but a sliver of it.

to the new reservation, as their former land now belonged to the United States. To pay for it, the U.S. Bureau of Indian Affairs promised to spend $265,000 on preparing 20-acre farms for the Indian families, to open tribal schools, and to allow the Indians use of government-financed sawmills and blacksmiths' shops. Soon, said the bureau, the Nez Perces could learn to stop wandering and start living a "civilized" life in the real American style. The bureau's definition of the good life, of course, bore no relation to the Indians' idea of spiritual and physical well-being.

Strengthening the Nez Perces' conviction that they had no right to sell land were the teachings of an Indian prophet who had begun attracting followers in the late 1850s. Smohalla was a hunchbacked member of the small Wanapum tribe who claimed he had died and been sent back by the Great Spirit to bring a message to the Indians. If the Indians listened to his message, he said, the whites would vanish, the buffalo would return, and all the Indians who had ever lived would come back to life.

Smohalla also maintained that the word of the supreme being was revealed to the faithful through dreams. "Dreamers," as Smohalla's believers came to be known, held not only that land could not be bought and sold but that it should not be farmed in the white man's way. At one point, the prophet expounded on his doctrines:

> My young men shall never work. Men who work cannot dream, and wisdom comes to us in dreams. . . . You ask me to plough the ground. Shall I take a knife and tear my mother's bosom? . . . You ask me to dig for stone. Shall I dig under her skin for her bones? . . . You ask me to cut grass and make hay and sell it and be rich like the white men. But do I dare cut off my mother's hair?

Several years after the signing of the Thief Treaty, Young Joseph gave his interpretation of the negotiations:

I believe that the old treaty has never been correctly reported. If we ever owned the land we own it still, for we
never sold it. In the treaty councils the commissioners have
claimed that our country had been sold to the Government.
Suppose a white man should come to me and say, "Joseph,
I like your horses, and I want to buy them." I say to him,
"No, my horses suit me, I will not sell them."

Then he goes to my neighbor, and says to him: "Joseph has
some good horses. I want to buy them, but he refuses to
sell." My neighbor answers, "Pay me the money, and I will
sell you Joseph's horses." The white man returns to me and
says, "Joseph, I have bought your horses, and you must let
me have them." If we sold our lands to the Government,
this is the way they were bought.

The Nez Perces positively resisted what they regarded
as the wrongful attempted seizure of their land, but they
bore no hatred for whites in general. Indeed, they made
many friends among the white pioneers, exchanging
visits, sharing celebrations, and racing their horses with
them. At the 1864 Fourth of July festival in the Grande
Ronde Valley, for example, Young Joseph and Ollokot
rode their handsomely painted horses in the parade, and
Old Joseph made a speech congratulating America.

When Old Joseph realized that the Americans really
intended to take his people's land, he was stunned.
Finally, he went to the trunk where he stored his most
precious possessions. From it, he took a copy of the Walla
Walla Treaty of 1855, along with a copy of the Bible,
and slowly tore them to pieces as his family looked on.
Then he mounted his horse, rode to the edge of the
Wallowa Valley, and built a fence across the trail. The
fence was not a warning but a message: this is Nez Perce
land; settlers, turn back.

Old Joseph's barrier failed to stop William H. Odell
and his government party from surveying the Wallowa
Valley. In his classic study, *The Nez Perce Indians and
the Opening of the Northwest*, author Alvin Josephy, Jr.,
reprints some of Odell's field notes.

This line passes through the beautiful Wallowa Valley [which is] about 6 miles wide and 40 long. . . . Narrow streams of clear cold water put down from the high snow mountains just to the South. . . . A large part of the Valley is well adapted to agriculture, while the low grassy hills to the N. and E. furnish extensive range for stock. The finest of trout and salmon abound in the streams, and many Indians camped upon the banks of the streams, taking great quantities of fish, while their large herds of horses quietly grazed upon luxuriant grass. This valley should be surveyed as soon as practicable, for the wigwam of the savage will soon give way to the [whites' homes]. Instead of the hunting and fishing grounds of the red man, the valley will teem with a thriving and busy population.

The elder Chief Joseph lived long enough to witness the beginning of the white invasion of his homeland. In May 1871, two cowboys drove their herds into the Wallowa Valley. Several other ranchers followed in their wake, setting up homesteads in the lush green valley. Merchants, farmers, and other white settlers soon moved into the Nez Perce country, and conflicts quickly began over land, water, and livestock.

Old Joseph had resisted the white invasion peacefully but persistently. He had told the whites again and again: "Our fathers were born here. Here they lived, here they died, here are their graves. We will never leave them." By 1871 he was an old man, blind and failing rapidly. Then one day, as Young Joseph was later to recall, Old Joseph called to him and spoke in a low voice:

My son, my body is returning to my mother earth, and my spirit is going very soon to see the Great Spirit Chief. When I am gone, think of your country. You are the chief of these people. They look to you to guide them. Always remember that your father never sold his country. You must stop your ears whenever you are asked to sign a treaty selling your home. A few years more, and the white men will be all around you. They have their eyes on this land. My son, never forget my dying words. This country holds your father's body. Never sell the bones of your father and your mother.

"I pressed my father's hand," Joseph said, "and told him that I would protect his grave with my life. My father smiled and passed away to the spirit land." Joseph's first duty as head of the Wallowa band of the Nez Perces was to inter his father. "I buried him in that beautiful valley of winding waters," he stated. "I love that land more than all the rest of the world. A man who would not love his father's grave is worse than a wild animal."

Joseph knew his father had deeply valued peace, and he did his best to preserve it. When white ranchers moved their herds directly onto the Wallowa band's traditional riverside pastureland, he visited the nearby town of Grande Ronde. He and his people had no wish for trouble, he told the whites. However, he said—for neither the first nor the last time—his band had signed the 1855 treaty that put the Wallowa Valley in their reservation. They had *not* signed the 1863 treaty, which gave away Indian lands. Therefore, said Joseph politely, would the ranchers please cease work on the new bridge and wagon road leading onto Nez Perce land?

The ranchers respected Joseph and his brother, and they, too, spoke courteously. But they pointed out that a "majority" of Nez Perce leaders had signed the 1863 treaty, and had accepted money or goods in exchange for land. Their government, they added, had opened the Wallowa Valley to them. They had spent time and money making it suitable for ranching, as they believed they had every right to do. They, too, wanted peace, and they hoped Joseph would ensure it. Meanwhile, they stayed put.

With the blessing of the whites (who thought the decision would favor them), Joseph brought the question to two government officials: John B. Monteith, the new Nez Perce Indian agent at Lapwai, and T. B. Odeneal, Oregon Indian affairs superintendent. Joseph outlined the

Indian agent John B. Monteith, originally sympathetic to the Nez Perces' claim to the Wallowa Valley, urged the government to abide by the Treaty of 1855. Embittered by the failure of his appeal, he ordered Joseph and his people to leave their homeland for a new, tiny reservation in Idaho.

situation with sharp clarity, and the government men grasped it quickly. "Each [race] considers the other a trespasser," they wrote in their report to Washington, "and the rash act of some imprudent white man, or reckless Indian, is liable to produce trouble at any time. We consider prompt action important."

The report continued: "If any respect is to be paid to the laws and customs of the Indians then the treaty of 1863 is not binding upon Joseph and his band. If so, then Wallowa Valley is still part of the Nez Perce reservation; this being the case, then the Government is equitably bound to pay the white settlers for the improvements and for the trouble, inconvenience and expense of removing from there."

No one wanted war, not Joseph, not the ranchers and settlers, not the government, and Monteith and Odeneal no doubt meant well. Working with Joseph, they devised a compromise that would have involved Indians and whites sharing the Wallowa Valley, a solution that would have satisfied both sides. But a series of errors, most of them originating with the bureaucracy in Washington,

D.C., was to make peace virtually impossible. The Wallowa Valley compromise was never realized; governors and representatives misunderstood and misrepresented not only each other but the settlers and Indians, too. Everyone, in short, ended up confused, disappointed, and angry.

The Nez Perce land tangle was the work of no one person or group, but Agent Monteith wound up as its scapegoat. Embittered by this injustice, he took his anger out on Chief Joseph and his people. In 1874, Monteith demanded that Joseph's band, along with all the other nontreaty Nez Perces, move to the reservation created by the 1863 treaty. A year later, the U.S. General Land Office decreed the entire Wallowa region open for settlement by non-Indians. The government ordered Joseph and his band to obey Monteith's orders, and to head for the crowded little Idaho reservation.

During the next two years, Chief Joseph and other nontreaty leaders took part in a number of councils with government representatives, each meeting following the same basic pattern. The government wanted the Indians to leave the territory they had allegedly sold to the government and to move—"for their own protection"—to the reservation, to take up farming, and to learn to live like whites.

The Indians wanted nothing of the kind. They wished to remain on the land of their ancestors, which they insisted they had never sold, and to maintain their traditional way of living. "We want to hunt buffalo and fish for salmon, not plow and use the hoe," said Joseph. "We do not plant; we harvest only the grain and berries that Mother Earth willingly gives us." Despite their directly contrary aims, however, Joseph still had no desire for war with the whites. Some Nez Perce leaders, including Joseph's brother, Ollokot, and Chief Looking Glass, agreed with Joseph, but others were less inclined

A Civil War veteran and postwar commissioner of the Bureau of Refugees, Freedmen, and Abandoned Lands, General Oliver Otis Howard listened with respect to Joseph's pleas for justice. He might have helped the Nez Perces, but the Sioux's 1876 annihilation of General George Armstrong Custer destroyed public support for Indians; in the end, Howard would travel almost 2,000 miles to catch Joseph and force him to obey U.S. regulations.

toward compromise. Eagle-from-the-Light, Toohoolhool-zote, and White Bird argued in favor of war.

It was at this time that Joseph first met General Oliver O. Howard, the new commander of the U.S. Army's Department of the Columbia. Although the two would soon be pitted against each other in one of the epic struggles for the American West, their first encounter was cordial. Howard, a 44-year-old career army officer who had lost an arm in the Civil War, saw himself as part soldier, part administrator, and part missionary. His piety had inspired the nickname by which most knew him: the Christian General.

Howard recalled that the Nez Perces came in to see him walking single file with Joseph in the lead. "One after another," he wrote, the Indians "took the agent's hand, and then mine, in the most solemn manner. Joseph put his large black eyes on my face, and maintained a fixed look for some time. It did not appear to me as an audacious stare; but I thought he was trying to open the windows of his heart to me, and at the same time endeavoring to read my disposition and character."

After hearing Joseph's arguments, Howard found himself deeply moved. "I think it is a great mistake," he wrote to the secretary of war, "to take from Joseph and his band of Nez Perce Indians that valley. The white people really do not want it. . . . Possibly Congress can be induced to let these really peaceable Indians have this poor valley for their own."

But it was not to be. Joseph's wishes—and those of Howard at that point—had small chance of being granted to start with, and the Sioux nation's stunning 1876 victory over General George Armstrong Custer meant those wishes would never come true. Custer, annihilated with his entire force by the Dakota Territory Indians in the celebrated Battle of the Little Bighorn, became a rallying point for the nation's anti-Indian movement. In deep mourning for the soldiers, the American public now demanded that the government corral all nonreservation Indians before they could do any more damage.

On January 6, 1877, Agent Monteith relayed his government's orders to Joseph: Leave the Wallowa Valley and take all your people to the reservation before April 1—or be forcibly taken there. "I have been talking to the whites for many years about the land in question," Joseph told Monteith, "and it is strange they cannot understand me. The country they claim belonged to my father, and when he died it was given to me and my people, and I will not leave it until I am compelled to."

Joseph talked boldly, but he was desperate for a solution. Finally, he requested a postponement of the departure date and a meeting with Howard. The general agreed, scheduling a conference for May 1877 at Fort Lapwai. Howard wanted to start talking as soon as Joseph arrived, but the Nez Perce chief wanted to wait for Chief White Bird and other leaders. Waiting would be unnecessary, said Howard; all the chiefs would receive the same orders: move to the reservation or face the U.S. Army. Describing his meeting afterward, Joseph said, "We were like deer. They were like the grizzly bears."

It was a stormy meeting, testing even Joseph's legendary calm. At one point, he looked straight at Howard and said, "Perhaps you think the Creator sent you here to dispose of us as you see fit. If I thought you were sent by the Creator I might be induced to think you had a right to dispose of me." Then, in a gentler tone, he added, "Do not misunderstand . . . my affection for the land. I never said the land was mine to do with as I chose. The one who has the right to dispose of it is the one who has created it. I claim the right to live on my land, and accord you the privilege to live on yours."

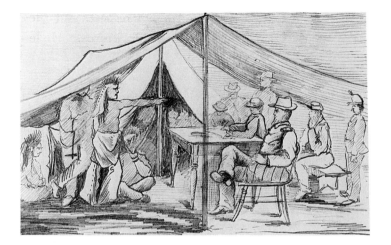

"You are trifling," says Toohoolhoolzote to Howard, "with the laws of the earth." Unmoved by the elderly chief's rage and pain, Howard locked him in the guardhouse and repeated his orders to the Nez Perces: Move to the new reservation voluntarily or be moved by force. Lieutenant Guy Howard, the general's son and aide, sketched the tense scene.

Adding to the meeting's tension was a crackling exchange between Howard and Toohoolhoolzote. Elderly, stubborn, and belligerent, Toohoolhoolzote challenged Howard at every turn. He talked at such length about the Indians' relationship with the earth that Howard, clearly at the end of his rope, at last interrupted him testily. "You do not propose to comply with the orders of the government?" he asked the chief.

"You are trifling with the laws of the earth," replied Toohoolhoolzote.

"Do the Indians want me to put them on the reservation by force?" snapped the increasingly exasperated general.

"I will not go," said the immovable Indian.

In the end, Howard "showed the rifle," as the Indians put it. He had Toohoolhoolzote locked up in the fort's guardhouse, and he gave Joseph 30 days to get his people onto the reservation. The chief now knew his band had to move. He helped his people assemble their animals and other possessions and hustled them along, speaking with hope and telling the younger men to stop promoting war. "It required a strong heart to stand up against such talk," he said later, "but I urged my people to be quiet, and not to begin a war."

Joseph's people held him in deep respect, and they followed him despite their anguish and bitterness. He led them east, across the torrential Imnaha, Snake, and Salmon rivers, toward Idaho. As they approached their destination, they decided to enjoy one last breath of freedom. Along with Looking Glass and White Cloud's bands, they made camp on the Camas Prairie, about a day's ride from the reservation. The decision to stop would prove both fateful and tragic.

4

THE WAR BEGINS

Joseph's people had left their homeland too hurriedly to round up all their stock. Behind them were not only hundreds of their cattle and horses, but many other possessions as well—ceremonial items, tipis, weapons, and food supplies—lost in the travelers' passage over turbulent rivers. The Indians lamented their vanished property, but their grief for the Wallowa Valley and their bitterness about the way they were forced to leave it knew no bounds. Joseph's band discussed their troubles with people in the other bands congregated on the prairie: those of White Bird, Toohoolhoolzote, and Red Owl—some 200 of them men, the rest women and children.

Joseph discouraged his people from dwelling on the past. Two weeks remained before they needed to report to the Lapwai Reservation, and he urged them to use the time gathering spring roots on the prairie and thinking of the future. Still, the encampment's voices returned again and again to the white men and their treatment of the Indians. As the days passed, the wanderers grew increasingly unhappy. Toohoolhoolzote spoke often, urging that his arrest by Howard be avenged. Some of the young warriors began to drink whiskey and to fire off their guns for no reason. Others drummed and sang all night long.

Looking Glass—who, like his father and namesake, always wore a small mirror at his throat—carries a bow and arrows as he prepares to leave his encampment. Hoping to keep out of General Howard's way, the Nez Perce chief refused to shelter White Bird and Toohoolhoolzote's bands after their young warriors' killing spree in June 1877.

One day in mid-June, Joseph gave his people another speech about maintaining peace, then checked on his pregnant wife, who was under the care of other women in a traditional birth tipi. (Indian custom allowed multiple marriages; Joseph would eventually have four wives.) Satisfied that things were under control, he rode off with his brother and brother-in-law to slaughter cattle for his band's food supply. The camp seemed calm.

The quiet did not last. Soon after Joseph departed, some of White Bird's warriors began to quarrel among themselves. One young man taunted another, hinting that he was a coward for not avenging his father's murder by a white man some years earlier. Already restless, angry, and probably intoxicated, the young man now vowed to kill that white. The next morning, June 13, he rode off to the Salmon River, followed by two of his friends. Unable to find his father's killer, the warrior settled for another white, a settler who had harassed Indians with his attack dogs. Then he and his companions hunted down and killed three more white men.

On June 14, when the three young murderers rode up on the dead settlers' horses, the rest of the camp immediately understood what had happened. One warrior leapt on a horse and galloped through the camp, shouting, "Now the soldiers will be after us! Prepare for war!" In almost no time, 17 young men—one of them from Joseph's band, the rest from White Bird's—applied war paint, mounted their ponies and joined the 3 who had just returned. Ready for blood and howling war cries, they thundered off to the settlements along Slate Creek, a small tributary of the Salmon River. At the same time, one of Joseph's headmen dashed off to find his leader, who returned at once to the camp. There, Joseph found only a scattering of tipis, evidence of a panicky departure, and a few Wallowa Nez Perces—including his wife and brand-new daughter. He learned that the rest of the

Warrior Wetyetmas Wahyakt strikes a formal pose in a photograph taken around 1930. More than half a century earlier, in June 1877, he and two other young hotheads massacred four whites along the Salmon River, triggering the Nez Perce War and nearly destroying the Nez Perce people.

Indians, except for the handful who had gone off to find victims, had packed their possessions and headed for the reservation.

White Bird and Toohoolhoolzote were showing their goodwill by leading their flocks to the reservation a day ahead of schedule. The chiefs planned to camp near Looking Glass's new village, hoping he would defend them against Howard; the general was sure to appear, furious and demanding to know about the Nez Perces' role in the Salmon River massacre. Famed as a mighty warrior, Looking Glass was also known to favor peace and to enjoy the whites' respect.

Meanwhile Joseph faced an agonizing decision: should he go to Howard at once, denounce the murders, and explain that only one of his people had ridden with the murderers? Or should he join the rest of the Indians from the camp, sharing whatever blame would fall? Years later, he recalled this time:

> I was deeply grieved. . . . I knew that their [the young warriors'] acts would involve all my people. I saw that the war could not then be prevented. . . . We had many grievances, but I knew war would bring more. . . . I would have given my own life if I could have undone the killing of white men by my people.
>
> I know that my young men did a great wrong, but I ask, Who was first to blame? They had been insulted a thousand times; their fathers and brothers had been killed; their mothers and wives had been disgraced; they had been driven to madness by the whiskey sold to them by white men. . . . They were homeless and desperate.
>
> I blame my young men and I blame the white men. I blame General Howard for not giving my people time to get their stock away from Wallowa. . . . I deny that either my father or myself ever sold that land. . . . It may never again be our home, but my father sleeps there, and I love it as I love my mother. I left there, hoping to avoid bloodshed.

Joseph had recognized a grim truth: war had begun. He knew it would bring suffering to all, particularly to the women and children, including his own infant daughter. But he also knew, he said, that he "must lead them in fight, for the white men would not believe my story."

As Joseph and his people regrouped on the Camas Prairie, warriors swooped down on the Slate Creek settlements, striking terror into the white community. Not yet informed about the raids, Joseph still had hopes of spiking the guns. If he and the other chiefs could arrange a meeting with Howard before any more shots

Framed by evergreens, Idaho's Camas Prairie supports a rich growth of camas, a type of lily whose roots the Nez Perces gathered for food. It was here at their old harvesting grounds that Joseph's band assembled in 1877, planning to enjoy a last breath of freedom before reporting to the Lapwai Reservation.

were fired, he thought they might be able to negotiate peace.

On their way to the reservation, Joseph's group met the hundreds of people who had recently left the Camas Prairie campsite. Turned away by Looking Glass—who wanted no part of this new trouble—White Bird, Toohoolhoolzote, and their bands were moving on to White Bird Canyon, site of one of White Bird's villages. Joseph and his group joined them.

Unknown to Joseph, however, Howard had already responded to settlers' calls for help. Believing that the murders were part of a general Nez Perce uprising rather than the act of a few revenge-seeking warriors, Howard had dispatched 105 cavalrymen to Mount Idaho, a town near White Bird Canyon. When the cavalry commander, Captain David Perry, learned that the Indians had headed for the canyon, he brought his men to the hill above it.

After riding more than 60 miles in 24 hours, the soldiers were bone tired; arriving at White Bird Hill in

White Bird Creek meanders along the canyon bottom where, on June 17, the Wallowa Nez Perces battled two companies of the First U.S. Cavalry. Commanded by Captain David Perry, the cavalrymen panicked and fired at the first sign of the Indians, provoking a wild skirmish that left 34 soldiers dead.

the early morning hours of June 17, most of them fell asleep as soon as they dismounted. Moments later, they heard a chilling sound. "There came from the timber the shivering howl of a coyote," recalled one of the soldiers. "That cry was an Indian signal, enough to make one's hair stand on end!" The army bugler sounded "boots and saddles," the signal to mount and prepare for battle.

As the soldiers advanced on the Indians, six Nez Perces rode out to meet them. According to some witnesses, the Indians carried a white flag of truce, indicating that they wished to talk, not fight. Other accounts make no mention of a flag. In any case, two Indians, trying to see what was happening, suddenly appeared on the hill behind the first group. The jittery soldiers spotted them, fired, and missed. Next, an Indian sharpshooter raised his rifle and downed the army bugler. Then the Indians sent a hail of bullets down the hill and the advance soldiers raced back to their main column.

The soldiers and their horses were exhausted even before they started fighting, but the Indians and their mounts were rested and fresh. Perry, with no bugler to relay his commands over the din of gunfire, was reduced to galloping through his ranks and screaming orders that no one heard. His men soon scattered in panic, leaving 34 dead and 3 wounded. The Indians had scored a complete victory—and now found themselves irretrievably at war.

The Nez Perces then had to decide what to do next. At this point, they knew Howard would never let them return to their homeland. Would he, they asked themselves, allow them to move onto the reservation land they had agreed to accept? Or would he pursue and punish them for their attack on the troops at the canyon? After lengthy conferences, they decided to move onto the reservation and settle near Looking Glass's territory.

The Nez Perces reasoned that if Howard came after them on the reservation, they could easily melt into the foothills of the Bitterroot Mountains, keep out of his reach, and meanwhile harass him with occasional surprise raids. Eventually, the Indians thought, Howard and the government he represented would want to end the state of hostility; they would ask for a peace conference, sign a treaty, and everyone could go on with their lives.

It was Joseph's task, as camp chief, to keep the group in order, to keep it moving, and to keep it safe. He had to calm the panicky, supervise the dismantling and packing of tipis and goods, and make sure the tribe's 2,500 horses were properly cared for. Joseph was also responsible for negotiating for his people, and for making plans for their future. He gave no orders: no Indian leader had the authority to order anyone to do anything. Each individual, each family, made its own decisions.

Even in battle, a warrior fought as he judged best and for as long as he felt like fighting. Neither Howard nor most other whites understood this facet of Indian leadership. To them, a group *must* have a leader. And in the case of the Nez Perces, Howard was sure he knew who the leader was. "The leadership of Chief Joseph was indeed remarkable," asserted Howard in his 1881 book, *Chief Joseph, His Pursuit and Capture.*

Joseph was a superb peacetime leader and a skilled negotiator for his people. Although he was also a stalwart warrior, distinguishing himself at White Bird Canyon and other battles, he neither planned nor led these fights. From White Bird on, many biographers and historians have portrayed him as the "Red Napoleon"—a military genius—but he was never a war chief. When it came time to fight, he listened to the advice and direction of such war leaders as White Bird, Rainbow, Looking Glass, Five Wounds, and Ollokot.

A formal portrait of Chief Joseph shows him holding a pipe, an important element in tribal councils and ceremonies. Although he was never the "Red Napoleon" legend has painted him, Joseph was a masterful negotiator, a natural peacetime leader, and—when war proved inevitable—a courageous warrior.

Most modern historians agree that the myth of Joseph as a great military strategist owes much to Howard. The general claimed he was up against a brilliant adversary, a military strategist who might have made Julius Caesar jealous. He portrayed Joseph in this manner partly because he really believed it and partly to justify his own lack of success in swiftly capturing the renegade Nez Perces.

After sending for reinforcements following the White Bird Canyon fight, Howard commanded 400 professional soldiers; far better, he must have thought, for the press to report him and his troops valiantly opposing a mighty chief than to be seen ineffectually chasing a band of some 550 noncombatants—women, children, and old people— and 250 warriors, led by a wise but unwarlike camp chief.

By late June, Joseph was leading the renegade Nez Perces toward the spot they had selected, doing his best to keep them as far from Howard as possible. The general, however, assumed that Joseph had sent word to other rebellious tribes, whose warriors might soon join him in an attack on the army. Thus when Howard received an untrue report—that Looking Glass and his people were sending supplies and warriors to the fleeing Nez Perces— he reacted with alarm. He ordered Captain Stephen Whipple to take two companies of cavalry to Looking Glass's village, lock all the Indians in a stockade near the town of Mount Idaho, and keep them there until he had dealt with Joseph's people.

When the soldiers reached the village on July 1, Whipple demanded that the Indians surrender. Looking Glass replied that they had done nothing to aid the rebels, that they had moved peacefully to the reservation, and that they should not be made prisoners. Then a nervous soldier suddenly fired into the Indian camp and pandemonium broke out. The people raced for the woods and the soldiers proceeded to burn the tipis, loot the camp, and drive off the horses. Enraged by this unjustified hostility, Looking Glass reassembled his people and led them straight to Joseph. Now Howard's fears became a reality.

In early July, when Howard found the Nez Perces encamped on the bank of the fast-flowing Clearwater River, he staged a surprise attack that sent the Indians fleeing. Howard considered the Clearwater battle a decisive victory—but he had not yet managed to capture Joseph. He hardened his resolve to stop the "war chief" and his people at any cost.

5

"PURSUE THE NEZ PERCES TO THE DEATH!"

The struggle between Indians and military produced countless acts of cruelty and courage on both sides. Most are lost to history, but one episode—a tale of heroism, mercy, and even humor—was recorded by a man who took part in it. He was Patrick Brice, a miner headed for the stockade at Mount Idaho in late June. On his way, he found a severely wounded seven-year-old white girl, Maggie Manuel. Her family, she managed to tell him, had been killed by Indians and their home burned to the ground.

The miner strapped Maggie to his back and continued his trek to town. He had just sighted the stockade when a party of Indians sprang from the woods. Brice dropped his gun and asked the warriors' leader to kill him if he must, but to let the little girl go. To Brice's surprise, the Indian said he could continue to town with Maggie, but only if he promised to return in two days. If he did not, said the warrior, "we will ride into Mount Idaho, and when we ride out again there will be no white person alive."

Brice agreed. He carried Maggie (who eventually recovered) to Mount Idaho, then—over the protests of incredulous settlers—returned to the Indians. This time, the man he faced was Chief Joseph. "Here I am," Brice recalled saying. "What are you going to do with me?"

Ollokot, Joseph's handsome younger brother and closest friend, gained enduring fame—among both whites and Indians—as a fearless and formidable warrior. One army wife described him as "a splendidly horrible looking Indian, over six feet and straight as an arrow."

"Do with you? Why, nothing," replied Joseph. "We do not want you. We are not making war on people who do not make war on us. It is the long knives [soldiers] we are fighting. Eat, sleep, then go your way." Brice did as told, speeding back to the town and its dumbfounded but cheering residents.

After the Clearwater battle, Joseph, Looking Glass, and the other Nez Perce leaders held a council to decide their next move. Looking Glass, an experienced warrior about 10 years older than the 37-year-old Joseph, insisted that all the nontreaty Indians head for Montana. It was the territory of the Crow Indians, he reminded them—the Crows, whom he had aided in their war with the Sioux, and who would surely aid their good friend now. The land teemed with buffalo and there would be plenty of food, plenty of hides. Most important for the fugitive Indians, said Looking Glass, the whites of Montana would no doubt prove friendly. After all, the Nez Perces had a quarrel only with the people of Idaho; those over the mountains would be cordial and welcoming.

Joseph had no use for this plan. In the first place, he considered Looking Glass somewhat unrealistic in expecting the whites to be friendly, and in the second, he wanted to go home. He believed that somehow, if the Nez Perces quietly returned to the Wallowa Valley, they could arrange peace with the whites. One of the men at the council later repeated Joseph's words to his fellow chiefs:

> What are we fighting for? Is it our lives? No. It is this fair land where our fathers are buried. I do not want to take my women among strangers. I do not want to die in a strange land. . . . We will put our women behind us in these mountains and die in our own land fighting for them. I would rather do that than run I know not where.

But Joseph found himself a minority of one. Even his close friends, the subchiefs Rainbow and Five Wounds, went along with Looking Glass and his plan. In the

A dense evergreen forest carpets the Bitterroot Mountains of eastern Idaho. In July 1877, Joseph led his people toward Montana and—they hoped—safety on the Lolo Trail, a dizzyingly steep, treacherous path winding through this rugged terrain.

Indian tradition, Joseph was free to do as he chose. But if he returned to the Wallowa Valley accompanied only by his immediate family, and if Howard caught him, he knew only too well what could happen: death at the end of a rope, an example to Indians who considered defying the whites. Joseph agreed to cross the Bitterroot Mountains of eastern Idaho into Montana.

The Indians planned their route: they would use the Lolo Trail, a narrow, windblown path that threaded its way through steep ravines, fallen trees, immense boulders, and patches of thick brush. Drenched by daily rains and nightly frosts even in mid-summer, the trail was treacherously muddy and slippery at its easiest; one false step and a person or animal would hurtle 2,000 feet into the rocky gorge below.

But the Nez Perces were accustomed to difficult travel. The men, women, children, and heavily loaded horses, along with the herd of unladen horses, made the punishing trip under Joseph's supervision with relative ease. By the end of July, they were on the Montana side of the mountains, straggling down the Lolo Trail toward the Bitterroot River.

At the trail's eastern end, however, the Indians met an unexpected obstacle. Running for a half-mile across the canyon at the base of the trail stretched a hastily built, hip-high log barricade. The wall was guarded by a company of soldiers under orders to stop the Indians and hold them until Howard's arrival. Riding ahead of their group and carrying a white flag, Joseph, White Bird, and Looking Glass approached the soldiers.

Through an interpreter, the Indians told the soldiers' commander, Captain Charles Rawn, that they intended no harm to anyone and that they simply wanted a peaceful passage into the Bitterroot Valley. With only 35 regulars and a company of volunteers under him, Rawn had no desire to battle 200 seasoned warriors. But he had his orders about the Indians from General Howard: "Prevent their escape."

The Nez Perces arranged several conferences with Rawn, but between meetings, they scouted exit routes from the canyon. On July 28, Joseph led his people on a steep, hidden path around the soldiers' barricade and toward the valley. The move took the soldiers completely by surprise. One of them, W. R. Logan, later described it.

> About 10 o'clock we heard singing, apparently above our heads. Upon looking up we discovered the Indians passing along the side of the cliff, where we thought a goat could not pass, much less an entire tribe of Indians with all their [possessions]. . . . Two civilians and I . . . followed the Indians for a mile or more. They were good-natured, cracked jokes, and seemed very much amused at the way they had fooled Rawn.

When the Nez Perce escape became known, the hapless Rawn faced the mockery of settlers, who tagged his barricade Fort Fizzle. But as the disconsolate Rawn watched the Indians heading east, another march was forming, this one headed west. On July 28, Colonel John Gibbon of the U.S. Army left his base on the opposite side of the mountains with a column of 150 foot soldiers and orders from General Howard to intercept the fugitives.

The Indians experienced no trouble crossing the valley. Realizing that they truly intended to make no trouble— and that they carried money to buy what they wanted— the valley settlers dealt with them peaceably, selling whatever supplies the Indians requested. From the valley, the Nez Perces proceeded across the Continental Divide (the highest peaks of the Rocky Mountains).

Once past the divide, they made camp at the Place of the Ground Squirrels, a pleasant, stream-crossed meadow in the center of a vast open basin of land called Big Hole. Arriving there on August 8, the Nez Perces breathed a collective sigh of relief. After the women cut tipi poles and the men pastured the horses, they held a feast of celebration, danced all evening, and finally fell asleep, feeling safe at last. They had left the war behind them. Or so they believed.

That night, just as the stars were fading, a column of men crept softly up the hilltop overlooking the Nez Perce camp. Colonel Gibbon, leading 146 soldiers, 17 officers, and a few dozen volunteers, looked down at the sleeping temporary village, a V-shaped group of 89 tipis. A dog barked, answering the distant howl of a coyote. Otherwise, all was quiet.

Satisfied that he had his quarry below him, Gibbon whispered his orders: the men were to form a long line, then move down the hill in absolute silence. At the signal, a rifle shot, they were to charge the Indian camp, guns blazing. As dawn broke, a single Indian rode toward the hill to check the horses pastured there. Three rifle shots

Colonel John Gibbon, a West Point graduate and distinguished Civil War veteran, led the attack on Joseph and his band at Big Hole, Montana, on August 9, 1877. Even after years of military experience, Gibbon found the events at the Big Hole uniquely grim. "Few of us will soon forget the wail of mingled grief, rage, and horror which came from the camp," he said later.

rang out. The Indian rider fell. The soldiers rushed forward, firing as they went.

Instantly, the air filled with screams, shots, and the sound of clubs on flesh. As the Indians' tied horses reared and whinnied and the camp dogs barked furiously, shocked warriors scrambled from their tipis, weapons in hand. Women, boys, and old people, too, seized whatever rifle or knife lay near and dived into the fight. The soldiers, recalled one participant, "shot every Indian they caught sight of—men, women, and children."

One Nez Perce warrior, Wounded Head, later described the scene as "hand to hand, club to club. All mixed up, warriors and soldiers fought. It was a bloody battle." As some of their officers fell, the soldiers broke ranks, allowing a wave of Indians to escape the camp. Following their orders, the soldiers tried to fire the tipis, but the tough hides refused to burn. As the men concentrated on their work of destruction, the warriors who had fled suddenly regrouped and charged back into the camp. Gibbon dispatched a runner to Howard, then shouted a call for retreat. His troops dashed for a rock ledge, dug in, and prepared to hold off the Indians.

Firing rapidly, the warriors kept the army pinned on the cliff while Joseph went to work. After rounding up the several hundred horses stampeded by the soldiers, he directed the camp's survivors to pack what was left of the tipis and load the wounded onto travoises. Then, through an atmosphere thick with the sounds of grief, he began to lead his people from the battle area. Joseph's nephew Yellow Wolf recalled the moment: "Wounded children screaming with pain. Women and men crying, wailing for their scattered dead! The air was heavy with sorrow. I would not want to hear, I would not want to see, again."

The sounds shook even Gibbon's battle-hardened soldiers. "Few of us," Gibbon recalled, "will soon forget the wail of mingled grief, rage, and horror which came from the camp four or five hundred yards from us when the Indians returned to it and recognized their slaughtered warriors, women, and children."

A silent cannon guards the hill above Big Hole battlefield, now a national monument. From this location, the 7th Infantry launched its assault on the sleeping Nez Perce encampment. The soldiers, recalled one survivor of the bloody encounter, "shot every Indian they caught sight of—men, women, and children."

Led by Joseph's brother Ollokot, the Nez Perce warriors covered the soldiers until Joseph had moved his band to relative safety. After dark, the warriors left, one by one, to join the rest of the group at an agreed-upon site some 12 miles distant. Now the tribe had time to count its dead. Lost were 33 men and 30 to 60 women, children, and babies—"the bitter fruit," says historian David Lavender, "of a simple desire to be left alone." (Lavender's acclaimed book, *Let Me Be Free: The Nez Perce Tragedy* appeared in 1992.) Among the women was Ollokot's wife. Joseph's two wives suffered serious injuries, but his baby daughter, born on the Camas Prairie only seven weeks earlier, survived without a scratch.

The Nez Perce bands now started on another long and difficult journey, slogging through western Montana, eastern Idaho, and northwestern Wyoming. Howard and his troops arrived at Big Hole only to learn that the Indians had escaped again. From that point on, they followed the Nez Perces relentlessly.

Using trackers, messengers, and scouts, the general set many traps for the Indians, stationing companies at trail

Nez Perce warrior Peopeo Tholekt drew this picture after the Big Hole battle. Although the Indians defended themselves with skill and courage, they lost scores of warriors and noncombatants—"the bitter fruit," says one historian, "of a simple desire to be left alone."

Howard rides alongside his men as they slog eastward, continuing their seemingly endless search for Joseph and his people. Stung by his superior's scorn—"If you are tired," said Army Secretary William Tecumseh Sherman, "give the command to some young, energetic officer"— Howard vowed to bring his pursuit of the fugitives to a "brilliant end."

points he was sure the fugitives would cross, but none of his ploys worked. Time after time, the Indians eluded the army. Here and there, advance cavalry columns traded fire with a few warriors, but after two exhausting months, the pursued continued to outrace their pursuers.

Howard appeared tireless, but his men were footsore, cold, underfed, and increasingly discouraged. The general now had to endure not only dark looks from his troops but scathing criticism from the press. The newspapers wanted to know why the army of the United States could not catch "an outnumbered bunch of Indians limping along burdened by women, children, and household possessions."

Howard's superior, Secretary of the Army William Tecumseh Sherman, was equally dissatisfied. "You should pursue the Nez Perces to the death, lead where they may," he wired. "If you are tired give the command to some young, energetic officer." Howard snapped back: "I never flag. . . . [I will] continue to the end." He vowed to bring the pursuit of the Nez Perces to a "brilliant end."

6

"I WILL FIGHT NO MORE FOREVER"

When the Nez Perce group—by now some 700 people, including several small bands that had joined the travelers on the way, and 2,000 horses—reached the Crow reservation in Wyoming, they met disappointment. The Crow chiefs treated their former allies with courtesy, promising to keep as many of their people as possible from siding with the army. Nevertheless, they said, they had no intention of bringing Howard's forces down on themselves; they would offer the fugitives no aid.

At this point, the Nez Perces, weary, hungry, and in many cases sick after trekking more than 1,000 miles, decided to head north to Canada. They believed they could find sanctuary with the Sioux chief Sitting Bull and his people, who had escaped to Canada after destroying Custer at the Little Bighorn. But in northern Montana, as the Nez Perce cavalcade neared the Canadian border, its leadership made a tragic mistake.

After Looking Glass had failed to foresee his people's ambush at Big Hole, the warrior-chief Lean Elk had taken over his job as war chief. Now, Lean Elk wanted to speed up the march and get out of Howard's range once and for all. Looking Glass disagreed. The group was now far ahead of its pursuers, he argued, and there was plenty of time to slow down and rest. He won general support and

After his people's flight and capture, Joseph's sorrowful expression seemed never to change. In this 1879 photograph, the Nez Perce leader wears his hair in the Dreamer religion style: cut short in front, stiffened and brushed straight up from the face.

took over his former position. Lean Elk agreed to go along with the majority, but with deep misgivings. "All right, you can take command," he told Looking Glass darkly, "but I think we will all be killed."

On September 28, the group made camp at the northern edge of the Bear Paw Mountains, 42 miles—a mere two-day ride—from the Canadian border. Looking Glass assured his comrades that they were safely ahead of Howard—and he was right. But he did not know the whole story: rapidly approaching the Bear Paws were 400 U.S. soldiers and 30 Indian scouts under the command of Colonel Nelson A. Miles. The troops were armed not only with rifles and small arms, but with two deadly high-wheeled cannons. Following Howard's orders, Miles intended to cut the Indians off before they reached the border.

On the morning of September 30, the Nez Perces were preparing to break their Bear Paw camp. Women were striking tipis and packing, men and boys rounding up and saddling their ponies. As he helped them, Joseph glanced up the hill at the edge of camp—and froze. There, outlined against the sky, a madly galloping scout waved a blanket furiously. Joseph instantly understood the message: The army is coming! Before any Indian could move, three units of the Second Cavalry, rifles blazing, charged the huge herd of Nez Perce horses. The animals screamed and plunged. Panic swept the camp.

In seconds, hundreds of Indians, their mounts already prepared to travel, fled the camp. Joseph was already in the saddle and racing for the herd, shouting "Horses! Horses! Save the horses!" In the midst of the shrieking confusion, he spotted his teenage daughter Kapkap Ponme (Sound of Running Feet) and signaled her to mount up and run with the others. He would catch up with her later, he yelled.

Nez Perce warrior-artist Peopeo Tholekt illustrated the Battle of the Bear Paws with a picture of himself (left, leading his horse) trading shots with one of General Miles's Cheyenne scouts. At this point, both sides were desperate: the Nez Perces to make their escape into Canada; the army to save face by capturing the renegades.

Then Joseph wheeled his horse back to the camp center. "I thought of my wife and children, who were now surrounded by soldiers," he said afterward, "and I resolved to go to them or die." Then, "with a prayer in [his] mouth to the Great Spirit Chief," he dashed through a storm of bullets to his family. "It seemed to me there were guns on every side, before and behind me," he continued. "My clothes were cut to pieces and my horse was wounded, but I was not hurt. As I reached the door of my lodge, my wife handed me my rifle, saying, 'Here's your gun. Fight!'"

By this time, Miles's cavalry and infantry units had thundered into the camp with what one Indian recalled as "a rumble like stampeding buffalo." The soldiers pounded the Indians with wave after wave of furious gunfire; the defenders—now about 75 warriors—returned a blistering fusillade. With his far superior numbers and weapons, Miles had expected to take the camp and its inhabitants in one charge, but the Indians fought his men to a standstill. He ordered another charge, this time hitting the Indians from both sides at once. Joseph's nephew Yellow Wolf later described the scene:

Bullets from everywhere. A big gun throwing bursting shells. From rifle pits, warriors returned shot for shot. Wild and stormy, the cold wind was thick with snow. A young warrior, wounded, lay on a buffalo robe, dying without complaint.

Joseph recalled it this way:

The soldiers kept up a continuous fire. Six of my men were killed in one spot near me. . . . We fought at close range, not more than 20 steps apart, and drove the soldiers back upon their main line, leaving their dead in our hands. We secured their arms and ammunition. We lost, the first day and night, 18 men and 3 women.

The death toll continued to rise. Among the fallen were people who had meant a great deal to the tribe—and to Joseph, whose beloved brother Ollokot lay dead on the battlefield. The warrior Lean Elk was dead, as were the tough old chief Toohoolhoolzote and a number of other warriors.

Snake Creek winds through the bleak meadow where the Nez Perces made camp on September 28, 1877. Here in the Bear Paw Mountains, the Indian band fought its last battle, a fierce, five-day struggle that cost the fugitives 22 lives—including those of Ollokut, Lean Elk, and Toohoolhoolzote—and their freedom.

Colonel Nelson Appleton Miles, commander of the army attack at the Bear Paws, was determined to capture the Nez Perces before General Howard arrived on the scene. Astounded when his first two charges failed, he finally laid siege to the camp and obtained the victory he had yearned for.

To Miles's amazement, the Indians held their ground against the army's powerful two-pronged offensive. Determined to win the battle before Howard arrived and got the glory, he pulled his men back and prepared to lay siege to the camp. Meanwhile, an earlier rain had turned into pelting, wet snow and the air had grown sharply cold. In the eerie silence that followed the army's pullback, the Indians tried to dig themselves in, scratching frantically at the hard earth with anything they could find—skillets, hunting knives, fingernails. But nothing could warm the shivering children or still their cries of hunger.

In the midst of the snow and howling winds, the crying and the death wails, Yellow Wolf dreamed of home. "Thoughts came of the Wallowa where I grew up," he recalled. "Of my own country when only Indians were there. Of tipis along the bending river. Of the blue clear lake, wide meadows with horse and cattle herds. . . . Then with rifle I stood forth, saying to my heart, 'Here I will die.'"

The next day, a soldier approached the Indian ranks with a white flag and a message: Colonel Miles wanted to talk to Chief Joseph. Never able to understand that the tribal system of government in no way resembled their own, Howard and other whites persistently treated Joseph as the head chief of all the Nez Perces as well as their war leader. Despite Miles's misunderstanding of Joseph's position, the surviving Nez Perce chiefs urged him to meet with Miles; he crossed the meadow between them at noon.

Miles got quickly to the point. The Indians were beaten, but if they surrendered unconditionally and gave up all their weapons, the army would escort them to Fort Keogh in eastern Montana. When the ice melted, they could move on to the Lapwai Reservation in Idaho—the site they had been approaching when the trouble began the previous June. No Nez Perce leader, added Miles, would be punished for any of the tribe's actions.

Joseph told Miles he did not represent all the Nez Perces, but he would tell them of Miles's offer. As for himself, he said, he would never agree to surrender all weapons. His people would need at least some of them to hunt for their food. When he finished speaking, he started back to the camp. The truce ended and Miles began shelling the Indian camp.

When Joseph described Miles's terms to his colleagues, some favored accepting them, others wanted to hold out, and still others wanted to slip away during the night. The majority rejected the last plan because it would have meant leaving their injured people behind. "We were unwilling to do this," noted Joseph. "We had never heard of a wounded Indian recovering while in the hands of a white man."

The battle resumed, intensified by the cannon that Miles had finally emplaced. The booming of the big gun added to the harsh crack of rifles, the whine of bullets, the groans of the wounded, and the cries of children. Weighting the air was the heavy smell of burned gunpowder. On the second day of the shelling, Looking Glass stood to sight his target and a bullet slammed into his brain, killing him instantly.

Joseph decided to surrender. "I could not bear to see my wounded men and women suffer any longer; we had lost enough already," he recalled. "Miles had promised that we might return to our country, with what stock we had left. I thought we could start again. I believed . . . Miles." White Bird, however, had no faith in the whites' promises. He refused to surrender, agreeing with Joseph that each should take his own path. The next day, White Bird escaped; with 104 followers, he arrived safely in Canada a few days later. Meanwhile, Howard and his force joined Miles.

Tom Hill (left), an English-speaking mixed-blood—half Nez Perce, half Delaware—Indian appears in a 1900 photograph with his friend Alec Hayes. Twenty-three years earlier, Hill had acted as Joseph's interpreter during his surrender negotiations with Miles.

On October 5, Joseph told his people—now including 87 men, 184 women, and 147 children—that he planned to surrender in their name. "Our people are out on the hills, naked and freezing. The women are suffering with cold, the children crying with the chilly dampness of the shelter pits," he said. "For myself I do not care. It is for them I am going to surrender."

That evening at sunset, Joseph mounted a black horse and rode up the hill to meet Howard and Miles. Five Nez Perce men walked beside their chief. Joseph wore his black hair in braids and, wrapped around his shoulders, a gray shawl riddled with bullet holes. He rode slowly, his hands crossed over the pommel of his saddle, his eyes downcast. When he reached Howard and Miles, he straightened, swung off his horse, and presented his rifle to Howard. The general motioned him over to Miles, who took the weapon from Joseph's outstretched hand. "From where the sun now stands," said Joseph in a low but clear voice, "I will fight no more forever."

"Indians, of course, possessed neither clocks nor calendars and generally used the imagery of the sun or moon to indicate the passage of time," notes historian Lavender. "Resorting to a common idiom meaning 'from now on,' Joseph [had] brought the story of a once-free people to a close."

Present at the surrender was Howard's aide-de-camp, Lieutenant Charles Erskine Scott Wood. According to Wood, who described the scene to a Dakota Territory newspaper three weeks later, Joseph handed over his rifle, then, through an interpreter, said:

> Tell General Howard I know his heart. What he told me before I have in my heart. I am tired of fighting. Our chiefs are killed, Looking Glass is dead. Toohoolhoolzote is dead. The old men are all dead. It is the younger men who say yes or no. He who leads the young men [Ollokot] is dead. It is cold and we have no blankets. The little children are freezing to death. My people, some of them, have run away into the hills and have no blankets, no food; no one knows where they are—perhaps freezing to death. I want time to look for my children and see how many of them I can find. Maybe I shall find them among the dead. Hear me, my chiefs; I am tired. My heart is sick and sad. From where the sun now stands, I will fight no more forever.

Yellow Wolf, Joseph's nephew, appears in full battle dress in this 1878 portrait. The Nez Perce warrior described the Bear Paws battle to author L. V. McWhorter, who published the by-then elderly Indian's memoirs as Yellow Wolf: His Own Story *in 1940. "Bullets from everywhere. A big gun throwing bursting shells," recalled Yellow Wolf. "A young warrior, wounded, lay on a buffalo robe, dying without complaint."*

For more than a century, Americans have found these words deeply moving. Where—or whether—Joseph really said them, however, has become a subject of heated debate. In his 1967 book, *The Flight of the Nez Perce,* historical researcher Mark H. Brown calls the speech a

"fiction" and says that if anyone can be credited with it, "that individual is probably Charles Erskine Scott Wood."

On the other hand, a number of western scholars—including Helen Addison Howard and Dan L. McGrath, authors of the widely read biography *War Chief Joseph* (1941; reprinted in 1971)—believe that Joseph gave the speech to a messenger, who relayed it to Howard before the surrender. Lavender writes that Wood may have inserted the speech into Howard's report to the secretary of war, basing Joseph's words on a message the Nez Perce leader had given to Howard's emissaries before the surrender. But although Wood may have invented all or part of the speech, it sums up what Lavender calls "the infinite sadness of a race's defeat and death."

At this point, Howard had pursued Joseph and his people for some 1,300 miles, but the Nez Perces, backtracking and circling to avoid capture, had covered more than 1,800 miles. Ill, cold, hungry, and weary to the bone, they were now prisoners of war. Under heavy military guard, they were to travel to Fort Keogh, Montana, where the army had decided they would spend the winter.

Soldiers drill on the Fort Keogh parade grounds in 1878. Colonel Miles designated the Montana outpost (later expanded and renamed Miles City) as the Nez Perces' 1877–78 winter quarters, promising to let the weary Indians rest, then move to the Lapwai Reservation in the spring. Like most other government promises made to Native Americans, this one would never be honored.

Ollokot's widow, Wetatonmi, later described this time. "Husband dead, friends buried or held prisoners. I felt that I was leaving all that I had but I did not cry," she said. "Strong men, well women, and little children killed and buried. They had not done wrong to be so killed. We had only asked to be left in our own homes, the homes of our ancestors. Our going was with heavy hearts, broken spirits."

7

"LET ME BE A FREE MAN"

In mid-October 1877, Joseph and the 418 surviving Nez Perces left the Bear Paw Mountains under military guard. With the well on horseback and the old and ill in travoises or wagons, the Indians and their military escorts made their way to isolated Fort Keogh, three days to the south. There, Colonel Miles noted in his memoirs, "the Nez Perce Indians were given a comfortable camp on the right bank of the Yellowstone [River] and it was my purpose to keep them there during the winter and send them back to [the Lapwai Reservation in] Idaho in the spring."

Miles genuinely respected his former adversaries. "The Nez Perces," he said in his official report on the Bear Paw battle, "are the boldest men and best marksmen of any Indians I have ever encountered." And of their leader, he wrote, "Chief Joseph is a man of more sagacity and intelligence than any Indian I have ever met; he counseled against the war, and against the usual cruelties practiced by Indians, and is far more humane than [the celebrated Sioux chiefs] Crazy Horse and Sitting Bull."

Reflecting their commander's attitude, Miles's troops treated their prisoners well, providing them with ample food, medical attention, and blankets. But six days after their arrival at Fort Keogh, Joseph learned that Miles had received new orders. Deciding that it would be too

This portrait of Chief Joseph, taken in Bismarck, Dakota Territory, in 1877, has been called the best likeness of the Nez Perce leader ever made. The Dakotans greeted Joseph warmly, clearly agreeing with Colonel Miles's description of Joseph as a man of "sagacity and intelligence" and a leader "far more humane than [Sioux chiefs] Crazy Horse and Sitting Bull."

expensive to maintain the captured Nez Perces at remote Fort Keogh, the Dakota Territory military commander wanted them moved out: Miles was to take them to Fort Abraham Lincoln, an outpost near Bismarck, North Dakota, 800 miles to the east. The Indians could spend the winter there.

On October 31, Joseph helped the women, children, and sick members of his group aboard a fleet of flatboats on the rapidly freezing Yellowstone River. Then he and the other able-bodied Indians, along with Miles and his cavalry, set out for Fort Lincoln on horseback.

Surprisingly, the people of Bismarck gave the arrivals a hero's welcome, embracing not only the victorious soldiers but the defeated Nez Perces. The Dakotans had read Joseph's (or Wood's) surrender speech, which apparently dissolved their traditional fear and hatred of Indians, and they greeted their visitors, white and red alike, with a "stampeed," as one eyewitness described it.

Bismarck (pictured in 1877), gave the Nez Perces a rousing reception. Moved by these proud people's plight, residents showered them with goodwill, food, and sympathy: "The devils," stormed one Bismarck woman, "to put those poor people under soldiers' guard!"

Entering the town on November 17, Miles's men formed a protective hollow square with the Indians inside. According to the eyewitness, "women children even men rushed the hollow squar with all kind of cooked food. . . . The command had to halt until each Nez Perce prisoner and even the over land guard was furnished with food of good kind." Two days after the Nez Perces' arrival, the *Bismarck Tri-Weekly Tribune* ran a front-page notice unlike anything ever seen, before or afterward, in the American West. Addressed to "Joseph, Head Chief of Nez Perces," the item read:

> Sir: Desiring to show you our kind feelings and the admiration we have for your bravery and humanity, as exhibited in your recent conflict with the forces of the United States, we most cordially invite you to dine with us at the Sheridan House in this city. The dinner is to be given at 1 1/2 P.M. today.

Joseph politely attended the dinner, where he found himself surrounded by the women of the town, all of them dressed in their finest clothes. Publicly, the solemn and dignified 37-year-old Nez Perce chief said nothing about his people's situation, but one sharp-eared diner later reported hearing him whisper a single mournful line: "When will the white men ever learn to tell the truth?"

But the Nez Perces were not to remain with the friendly citizens of Bismarck. Miles, no doubt sincerely, had promised Joseph that he and his people could return to Idaho in the spring. But he had been overruled. When news of the Indian defeat at the Bear Paws had reached Idaho, settlers there set up an immediate and passionate protest against the tribe's reappearance.

Idaho's public prosecutor responded to the whites' protests by having Joseph and 34 other Nez Perces indicted for murder—wrongly blaming them for the killings by White Bird's warriors at Slate Creek. Asserting that the Nez Perces would be shot on sight in Idaho, the regional inspector for the Bureau of Indian Affairs then recommended that they be sent "so far away that they can never return." Secretary of the Army Sherman agreed. Miles, he said, had not been authorized to promise to send the Nez Perces home or, indeed, to promise them anything. Sherman commanded Miles to requisition a train, load the rebel Indians aboard, and take them at once to faraway Fort Leavenworth, Kansas.

Before the departure, a local white man tried to tell the Indians about trains, an invention none of them had ever seen. He described "the great Iron Horse that had the speed of a hundred ponies that lived on wood and water"; it made great noises, he said, but would not hurt them. Nevertheless, the Indians regarded the railroad in terror, boarding the cars of the Northern Pacific Railroad with great reluctance. As the train pulled out, Joseph stood on the rear platform, waving to the friendly crowd assembled at the depot, but in the cars behind him, many of his people cried. Some, reported a witness, began moaning in what he assumed was "their death chant." Thus they rolled on into deeper exile.

Joseph and his people arrived at Fort Leavenworth on November 24, 1877. The soldiers placed them in an area between a swamp and the Missouri River, some two miles north of Fort Leavenworth. Despite bitter cold, the winter proved uneventful, but the spring brought new tragedies. Swarming mosquitoes from the swamp spread malaria, and by July, 21 people, most of them children, were dead. "I cannot tell how much my heart suffered for my people while at Leavenworth," Joseph said later. "The Great Spirit Chief who rules from above seemed to be looking some other way, and did not see what was being done to my people."

Observing what he called the "simply horrible" state of the Nez Perces, a Civil War veteran in Miles's regiment wrote about "the 400 miserable, helpless, emaciated specimens of humanity" in the Indians' camp. "They

An 1877 bird's-eye shot of Fort Leavenworth, Kansas, shows rows of drab military structures set in a bleak, treeless plain—a landscape utterly unlike the Nez Perces' lush, forested homestead. Racked by illness and despair, Joseph's people died in shocking numbers at Leavenworth.

presented a picture," he said, "which brought to my mind the horrors of Andersonville [a notorious Civil War Confederate prison]. One-half were sick, principally women and children. All were filled with the poisonous malaria of the camp."

Joseph never stopped agitating for the right of his people to return to their homeland, but his efforts continually ran into a stone wall. The Bureau of Indian Affairs (which had succeeded the army as the Nez Perces' supervisors) had no intention of letting the Indians return to the Northwest. Bureau officials asserted that white hostility and the murder indictments against Joseph and his colleagues made such a move too dangerous.

In truth, however, Howard was once again pursuing fugitive tribes in the Northwest—this time the Northern Paiutes and the Bannocks—and the Sioux were showing new signs of hostility. The BIA believed that the reap-

pearance of Joseph and his people might act as a unifying
force for these restless people, and might even trigger
new Indian wars. But Joseph's constant pleas, along with
those of Miles and even the commandant of Fort Leavenworth, finally produced some action: in July 1878, the
bureau announced that it would resettle the Nez Perces
on 7,000 acres in the Quapaw Reservation in southeastern
Kansas.

The Kansas site proved no healthier or happier for the
Nez Perces. The soil was poor and the water supply
inadequate; two months after the Indians' arrival, 47 more
people had died. Meanwhile, the rest of the nation had
begun to take notice of the Nez Perces' plight. The speech
attributed to Joseph had been widely reprinted and much
admired, and the remarkable actions of the people of
Bismarck had piqued general interest in the Nez Perces.
BIA executives knew they had to make some move to
avoid a storm of public criticism.

Finally, BIA commissioner Ezra Hayt decided to take
action himself. In the fall of 1878 he made a special trip
to Kansas to talk to Chief Joseph. Hayt told him that
Indian hostilities in Idaho absolutely ruled out a return
to the area, but that Joseph could have his pick of spots
in a broad sweep of lands in Kansas, Arkansas, and
present-day Oklahoma. Joseph toured the area with the
commissioner, eventually selecting a 90,000-acre plot in
Indian Territory (Oklahoma).

The Nez Perce chief made a strong impression on the
Indian commissioner. "I found him to be one of the most
gentlemanly and well-behaved Indians I ever met," Hayt
commented later. "He is bright and intelligent and is
anxious for the welfare of his people. . . . Care should be
taken to place them where they will thrive." Hayt not
only made arrangements to buy the Oklahoma land but
also arranged a visit for Joseph to Washington, D.C.

There, said Hayt, Joseph could tell his story to President Rutherford B. Hayes himself, as well as to Secretary of the Interior Carl Schurz.

Accompanied by an interpreter, Joseph and his friend Yellow Bull arrived in the capital in early 1879. Joseph's interviews with the president and interior secretary must have been short and routine; no official record of them remains. But on January 14, the Nez Perce leader addressed a large audience at Washington's Lincoln Hall, an event that was neither routine nor unrecorded.

With his hair in tight braids and wearing a striped blanket coat, several bead necklaces, and beaded moccasins, Joseph mounted the platform and faced the crowd. "Some of you think an Indian is like a wild animal," he began. "This is a great mistake. I will tell you all about our people, and then you can judge whether an Indian is a man or not." Joseph captured his audience with his first words, then kept it spellbound for two hours. (His time on the stage was doubled by the need for translation.)

Joseph summarized the history of Nez Perce contacts with whites, starting with explorers Lewis and Clark, then going on to Lawyer's unauthorized "sale" of tribal lands in 1863 and Miles's unfulfilled promises. Discussing the whites' many broken pledges, Joseph's voice rose slightly.

> I have heard talk and talk and nothing is done. . . . Good words do not last long until they amount to something. . . . Words do not pay for my dead people. They do not pay for my country, now overrun with white people. They do not protect my father's grave. . . . Good words will not give me back my children. . . . Good words will not give my people good health and stop them from dying. Good words will not get my people a home where they can live in peace and take care of themselves.

As Joseph neared the end of his speech, his audience sat riveted. Not a cough, not a rustled program, hardly a

breath stirred the packed hall as he spoke his final words for the day.

> I know my race must change. We cannot hold our own with the white men as we are. We only ask an even chance to live as other men live. We ask to be recognized as men. We ask that the same law shall work alike on all men. . . .
>
> Let me be a free man—free to travel, free to stop, free to work, free to trade where I choose, free to choose my own teachers, free to follow the religion of my fathers, free to think and talk and act for myself—and I will obey every law or submit to the penalty.
>
> Whenever the white man treats the Indian as they treat each other, then we shall have no more wars. We shall be all alike—brothers of one father and one mother, with the sky above us and one country around us, and one government for all. Then the Great Spirit Chief who rules above will smile upon this land, and send rain to wash out the bloody spots made by brothers' hands upon the face of the earth. For this time the Indian race are waiting and praying. . . .
>
> Hin-mah-too-yah-lat-kekht has spoken for his people.

Eloquent but soft-voiced, proud but willing to change, gentle of manner but immovable in purpose, Joseph had all but hypnotized his listeners. A moment of dead silence followed his speech; then came a crashing roar of applause and cheers. Two months later, a translation of Joseph's words, entitled "An American Indian's View of Indian Affairs," appeared in the influential magazine *The North American Review*. Thousands of people read it and suddenly understood the enormous injustice inflicted on the Nez Perces.

But still no one acted. No offical or agency made plans to help the Nez Perces return to their beloved Oregon or even to the Lapwai Reservation in Idaho. Disappointed yet again, Joseph and Yellow Bull returned to the Quapaw tract. The following July, Joseph supervised his people's move to the 90,000 acres the government had bought for them near present-day Tonkawa, Oklahoma.

Posed near a stack of artificial boulders, Nez Perce chief Yellow Bull wears a borrowed coat in this 1879 studio portrait. When he and Joseph visited Washington, D.C., local photographers insisted on dressing them in stereotyped "aboriginal" getups, none of which resembled the Indians' real-life attire.

Born and raised in the cool mountain country of Oregon, the Nez Perces found Oklahoma's dry, flat terrain and broiling temperatures almost unbearable; they called their new quarters Eeikish Pah—"Hot Place." People sickened and died; not one Nez Perce infant born there survived. Joseph's own daughter, the baby born near the Camas Prairie in June 1877 and cradled in her father's arms during the Battle of the Big Hole, was among the youngsters who died in Eeikish Pah. To a visiting official, Joseph had this to say:

> You come to see me as you would a man upon his deathbed. The Great Spirit above has left me and my people to their fate. The white men forget us, and death comes almost every day for some of my people. He will come for all of us. A few months more and we will be in the ground. We are a doomed people.

The Nez Perces' anguish failed to move the U.S. government, but the Indians had friends, and Joseph's widely circulated Lincoln Hall address had created an ever-expanding group of advocates. Miles had embarked on a one-man crusade of letter writing, urging everyone he knew in official circles to help the Nez Perces return to their homeland. Howard's former aide, Charles Erskine Scott Wood, was also active on the Indians' behalf. Several white organizations, including the new Indian Rights Association and the Presbyterian church, undertook petition campaigns for Joseph's band.

The intense public pressure finally produced action. In 1883, Congress allowed 29 Nez Perce widows and orphans to move to Kamiah, part of Idaho's Lapwai Reservation. Now that they had begun to act, the legislators kept on. On July 4, 1884, they passed the Indian Appropriation Bill, authorizing the Interior Department to release the captive Nez Perces from Indian Territory.

President Rutherford B. Hayes appeared sympathetic when he met with Joseph in 1879, but he made no move to help the beleaguered Nez Perces. "I have seen the Great Father Chief [Hayes] . . . and many other chiefs, and they all say they are my friends," said Joseph, "but while their mouths all talk right, I do not understand why nothing is done for my people."

The Indians, decreed the department, could return to the Northwest—although not to the Wallowa Valley. Officials feared that with ongoing white hostility and the outstanding murder indictments against Joseph and his colleagues, such a move could stir up a hornet's nest. The Nez Perces would be split into two groups, 147 people going to Lapwai and 150 going to Nespelem, an area of the Colville Reservation in northern Washington Territory.

A glum quintet of Nez Perce women join an equally grim-faced man outside a tipi at the Colville Reservation in Washington State. When they realized that the displaced Nez Perces would not take up the ways of white people, the reservation's Indian agents sneered. "It isn't as if these savages had not been given every chance to learn," said one.

8

KOPET

After the Battle of the Bear Paws, the army had interned almost 500 Nez Perces. Disease and despair, however, had claimed some 40 percent of those people during the following seven years; departing Eeikish Pah in the spring of 1885 were only Joseph and 295 other survivors. As they boarded the wagons, a mournful wail pierced the air. The Nez Perces were leaving their dead in a foreign place.

Because Washington's Colville Reservation was closer to their Oregon homeland than was Idaho's Lapwai, Joseph and his Wallowans settled in Colville's Nespelem area. The return to the West stirred Joseph. "If I could," he said, "I would take out my heart and hold it in my hand and let the Great Father and the white people see that there is nothing in it but kind feelings and love for Him and them." But the Nez Perces soon discovered that even here, they were strangers. The Interior Department had already settled several other tribes near Nespelem, and these people had no wish to share their territory with the Nez Perces. Only the intervention of federal troops made it possible for Joseph and his band to move into the region.

For centuries, the Nez Perces had lived by hunting, fishing, raising horses, and gathering roots and wild plants. The Colville agent expected them to take up farming, but the Indians believed it improper to take more than the earth gave freely; they had never farmed and they had little interest in starting now. Instead, most of them made a meager living by working as day laborers on roads and construction sites, picking hops in the Yakima Valley to the south, or applying for small sums from the Bureau of Indian Affairs.

Adding to the general gloom of life at Colville was the attitude of the reservation's Indian agents. Over the years, some administrators would prove honest and sympathetic, but many felt deep contempt for all Indians and cheated them regularly. Colville agent Albert Anderson was one of the second variety. In a typical report to BIA headquarters, Anderson wrote as follows:

> No tribe under the jurisdiction of this agency has received the attention and assistance from the Government that Chief Joseph and his band have. Regardless of this . . . they have been persistent in following their ancient traditions and indulging in their primitive customs. . . . Their dress on frequent occasions is hideous in appearance and possesses many of the characteristics of the Indian in his native state.

> They have no religion, believe in no creed, and their morality is at a low ebb. . . . Closer restrictions should be thrown around them. . . . Chief Joseph, with his handful of unworthy followers, prefers . . . living on the generosity of the Government and passing away their time in a filthy and licentious way of living.

Lavender observes that in using the word *licentious*, Anderson probably particularly referred to Joseph's having two wives, as did most of his peers. His first wife had been killed in the war and his second had elected to live at the Lapwai Reservation rather than Colville. When he arrived at Colville, Joseph had followed the common practice of marrying the widows of a fallen warrior, in this case Looking Glass. The move had deeply displeased

Anderson. When told he should divorce one of his wives, Joseph replied that the whites had taken his country but that he would keep his wives.

And in his use of the word *filthy*, Anderson was mistaken: Joseph's wives reportedly kept his home immaculate. "The interior of Chief Joseph's tepee," wrote one white visitor to Colville, "presents a model appearance of neatness. Indian mats cover the floor and in huge rolls around the edge are buffalo robes now quite scarce among the Indians, and blankets."

Disheartened by life at Colville, many of the young men spent too much of their small incomes on liquor, deeply saddening Joseph. He had always regarded alcohol as an enemy of his people and never drank himself, hoping—usually in vain—to set a good example. As time passed, however, the Nez Perces adjusted to Nespelem, finding new hunting grounds and fishing streams and raising and racing horses. But Joseph, often described by white visitors as "friendly" but "sad," never lost sight of his dream.

In 1897, non-Indian prospectors began drifting into the southern part of the Colville Reservation, and Joseph decided to use their trespassing to reopen the Wallowa question. Once again, he made the long journey to Washington, D.C. There, he spoke to President William McKinley, who seemed sympathetic but who promised nothing. In the East, Joseph also met the newly promoted general Nelson Miles, who invited his old foe to accompany him to New York City.

Aware that publicity could help his cause, Joseph joined Miles in dedication ceremonies for the tomb of Ulysses S. Grant—ironically, the president whose Indian policy had pushed the Nez Perces out of the Wallowa Valley. In New York, the Nez Perce leader agreed to pose for a picture with Buffalo Bill Cody, the celebrated cavalry scout and "Wild West" showman. Asked later for his opinion of Joseph, Cody called him "the greatest Indian America ever produced."

The New York newspapers had a field day with Chief Joseph, reporting his every move to their eager readers. The Nez Perce leader, note biographers Helen Howard and Dan McGrath, "was besieged by Easterners who were thrilled to get sight of or talk to a genuine, 'honest-to-gosh' red Indian chief out of the wild and woolly West,

Joseph (left) shakes hands with the legendary Buffalo Bill Cody, onetime cavalry scout turned "Wild West" showman, in 1900. Cody, who counted many Indians among his friends and acquaintances, called Joseph "the greatest Indian America ever produced."

who had actually led his tribespeople on the warpath against the American army."

One reporter wrote of an encounter between Joseph and a fashionable New York woman. Peering at him from under an immense feathered hat, she asked, "Did you ever scalp anybody?" Joseph seemed to suppress a smile. He considered the question, then turned to his interpreter and pointed to the woman's hat. "Tell her," he said, "that I have nothing in my collection as fine as that."

Clearly, Joseph had captured the popular imagination. Powerful people—Miles, the widow of President James Garfield, even General Howard—now supported his cause. The Bureau of Indian Affairs even promised a new investigation into Nez Perce claims on the Wallowa

Valley. Still, no one actually *did* anything. When Joseph left the East Coast, it was once again with empty hands.

Since May 1877, when he led his people out of the valley and toward Idaho, Joseph had never laid eyes on his homeland. Told by BIA officials and others that his appearance there could seriously harm his cause, he had stayed away from the valley for almost a quarter of a century. But in 1899, he made up his mind to return. He would talk to the whites who had settled in the area and get some figures on current land prices. Perhaps, he thought, that information might spur the BIA into action at last.

After obtaining the agency's permission to visit the Wallowa Valley, the 60-year-old Joseph traveled to Oregon. Now crisscrossing the magnificent, once-wild valley were irrigation ditches, fences, ranches. Along the winding river were four small towns—one of them named Joseph. But in spite of the changes, the craggy peaks remained; the grassy plains, dark evergreen forests, and sparkling river remained. The cool wind still blew,

Tall peaks rise above Joseph, Oregon, a town built by settlers on lands that once belonged to the Nez Perces. Although they had given the community his name, the whites refused to give Joseph the right to return to the Wallowa Valley with his people.

and horses still grazed where Nez Perce horses had grazed. This was home.

By this point, Joseph was the valley's most famous son. General Oliver Howard had written a book about the Nez Perce's brilliant military tactics, presidents of the United States had met with him, Buffalo Bill had described him as America's "greatest Indian." Eager to see this phenomenon in person, the valley's white residents called a public meeting. The settlers gave Joseph a warm welcome—until he announced that he and his people hoped to return to the Wallowa Valley.

First, Joseph pointed out that the Nez Perces had never signed over their land in a treaty. Then he asked if the settlers would consider selling—for a good price—a small tract of that land to the BIA, which would hand it back to the Nez Perces. The white faces froze. One of the ranchers responded for the others.

The Nez Perces had given up rights to the land, said the rancher, when they left it and went to war against the United States. The settlers had acquired their homesteads and ranchlands in good faith from the government, and they had worked hard to improve them. The last thing they wanted was a tribe of Indians—known troublemakers at that—in their midst. The whites would never sell a single acre to the Indians. They should forget about returning, now or ever.

Along with his people, Joseph had endured 24 years of punishing exile, and he refused to give up his cause now. The white man's desire for vengeance had to be satisfied sometime; sooner or later, the government would have to stop treating the Nez Perces as prisoners of war. In 1900, the BIA responded to Joseph's constant pleas by dispatching an inspector, James McLaughlin, to take a firsthand look at the situation.

"My home is in the Wallowa Valley, and I want to go back there to live," Joseph told McLaughlin. "My father

Wearing a war bonnet, Joseph inspects his tipi, his two horses, and the small plot of land assigned to him at the Colville Reservation. It was here that the Nez Perce leader lived for 19 years, and here that he died, aged 64, on September 21, 1904.

and mother are buried there. If the government would only give me a small piece of land for my people in the Wallowa Valley, with a teacher, this is all I would ask." Joseph returned to the valley with McLaughlin, this time receiving a chilly reception from the settlers. After listening to the unrelenting ranchers and farmers, Mc-Laughlin wrote an official report recommending that Joseph and his people remain on the Colville Reservation.

Joseph made a few more half-hearted efforts to get action, but he had finally lost hope. He knew now that he and his people would never again live in the Wallowa Valley. Joseph spent most of the next five years at the Colville Reservation, where, refusing to occupy the wood-framed house the government had built for him, he lived in a tipi. It was there, as he sat by his small fire on September 21, 1904, that the gallant Indian leader died. Modern medical authorities attribute Joseph's death to a massive heart attack. But reservation doctor Edward H. Latham, who had been his physician and friend for 14 years, perhaps knew better. "Chief Joseph," he said, "died of a broken heart."

The next day, the Nez Perce community quietly buried its chief with traditional prayers and chants. The following June, Joseph's body was reburied in Nespelem during an elaborate ceremony attended by both Indians and whites. Joseph's friend Yellow Bull, aged and nearly blind, gave the main speech.

Astride Joseph's faithful old horse and wearing Joseph's spectacular, six-foot-long eagle-feather warbonnet, Yellow Bull circled the grave site three times. At last, pausing by Joseph's tall white marble monument, the old warrior talked of his friend and of his 1879 speech in Lincoln Hall. "Joseph is dead but his words will live forever," he said. "Joseph's words will stand as long as this monument."

After Yellow Bull's speech, noted one reporter, "The mourners encircled the grave. A high-keyed, falsetto chant by forty voices, rising and falling in absolute unison, sent chills down our spines that hot June day, as does the dismal wail of wintry winds in the pine forests."

One of Joseph's white admirers, photographer-writer Edward S. Curtis, covered the funeral for *Scribner's Magazine*:

On the [day after the interment], came the Chief Joseph potlach (Big Giving), in which every earthly possession of the old chief and his wife was given away . . . and so closed the last chapter in the life and death of the most decent Indian the Northwest has ever known. . . . His troubled life has run its course, and one of the greatest Indians who ever lived is no longer.

This was the closing act in the drama of the life of Joseph, the last of the Nez Perce "non-treaty" chiefs. To employ words in condemnation of the great wrong that his people suffered would be useless, for was it not but one of the countless iniquities that have marked the white man's dealings with the Indians since the landing of the Pilgrims at Plymouth?

As Joseph himself would have said at this point, "*Kopet*"—in his language, "That is all."

To many of Joseph's white contemporaries, he was the Red Napoleon, a military genius of astonishing skill. Even today's western histories often identify him as War Chief Joseph. His military reputation, of course, was largely the creation of General Howard, who needed the vision of a formidable opponent to justify his slowness in capturing the renegade Nez Perces. But in truth, Joseph *was* a remarkable leader.

No single chief, of course, ruled the Nez Perces, but it was Joseph who kept his people going, who inspired them

At a 1905 memorial service in Nespelem, Washington, Yellow Bull faces the monument dedicated to Chief Joseph. Referring to his old friend's celebrated speech—"Let me be a free man . . ."—in Washington, D.C., Yellow Bull said, "Joseph is dead, but his words will live forever."

to make one of the most extraordinary human flights in history. Joseph helped pilot his people through three territories—across 1,800 miles of towering mountain ranges, steep canyons, turbulent rivers, and rocky plains. Vastly outnumbered and outgunned by the U.S. Army, the Nez Perces outmaneuvered and outfought their opponents until the very end.

But Joseph's lasting fame rests less on his remarkable leadership than on his extraordinary spirit. It is as a defender of human liberty and dignity that he stands tallest in American history. Unflaggingly true to his principles, Joseph pursued what he saw as his people's inalienable rights—indeed, as all people's rights. He championed peace, brotherhood, and—perhaps most important of all to him—freedom.

> If the white man wants to live in peace with the Indian, he can live in peace. There need be no trouble. Treat all men alike. Give them all the same law. Give them all an even chance to live and grow. All men were made by the Great Spirit Chief. They are all brothers. The earth is the mother of all people, and all people should have equal rights upon it.

> You might as well expect the rivers to run backward as that any man who was born free should be contented penned up and denied liberty to go where he pleases. . . . Let me be a free man—free to travel, free to stop, free to work, free to trade where I choose, free to choose my own teachers, free to follow the religion of my fathers, free to think and talk and act for myself—and I will obey every law, or submit to the penalty.

CHRONOLOGY

1840   Born in Wallowa Valley, near present-day Oregon-Washington border

1855   Attends Walla Walla council with father and other Nez Perces; Indians and U.S. government sign Treaty of 1855

1860   Joseph marries first wife; gold rush spills over into Nez Perce land

1863   Joseph attends council but refuses to sign "Thief Treaty" of 1863, which cedes 7 million acres of Nez Perce land to the U.S. government

1874   U.S. government opens Nez Perce lands to public settlement; orders Indians to move to a reservation in Idaho

1877   Joseph, hoping to keep peace, leads Nez Perces toward Idaho; murder of settlers ignites Nez Perce War; Joseph and his band make an 1,800-mile dash for freedom; Joseph surrenders to U.S. Army; exiled, along with his people, in Fort Leavenworth, Kansas

1878   Sent with his band to Quapaw Reservation in present-day Kansas

1879   Visits Washington, D.C.; meets President Rutherford Hayes and makes speech appealing for Nez Perce rights; returns to Midwest; helps his band move to Eeikish Pah reservation in present-day Oklahoma

1884   With part of the exiled Nez Perce group, moves to Colville Reservation in Washington Territory; marries the two widows of a fallen warrior; continues to fight for Nez Perces' right to return to Wallowa Valley

1897   Again travels to Washington, D.C., this time to plead with President William McKinley for his people's homeland; returns to Colville empty-handed

1899   Visits Wallowa Valley; tries, vainly, to persuade settlers to allow return of his people

1900   Makes second futile trip to Wallowa Valley

1904   Dies at Colville on September 21

FURTHER READING

Beal, Merrill D. *I Will Fight No More Forever*. Seattle: University of Washington Press, 1963.

Brown, Mark. *Flight of the Nez Perce*. Lincoln: University of Nebraska Press, 1967.

Freeman, Russell. *Indian Chiefs*. New York: Holiday House, 1987.

Gidley, Mick. *Kopet: A Documentary Narrative of Chief Joseph's Last Years*. Chicago: Contemporary Books, Inc., 1981.

Howard, Helen Addison, and Dan L. McGrath. *War Chief Joseph*. Lincoln: University of Nebraska Press, 1964.

Howard, Oliver O. *Nez Perce Joseph*. 1972.

Josephy, Alvin M., Jr. *Chief Joseph's People and Their War*. Yellowstone National Park: Yellowstone Library and Museum Association, 1964.

Lavender, David. *Let Me Be Free: The Nez Perce Tragedy*. New York: HarperCollins, 1992.

McWhorter, L. V. *Hear Me, My Chiefs!* Caldwell, ID: Caxton, 1952.

————. *Yellow Wolf: His Own Story*. London: Abacus, 1977.

Schwantes, Carlos A. *The Pacific Northwest: An Interpretive History*. Lincoln: University of Nebraska Press, 1989.

Slickpoo, Allen P., Sr., and Deward E. Walker, Jr. *Noon-Me-Poo*. Lapwai, ID: Nez Perce Tribe of Idaho, 1973.

Trafzer, Clifford E. *The Nez Perce*. New York: Chelsea House Publishers, 1992.

Trafzer, Clifford E., and Richard D. Scheurman. *Chief Joseph's Allies*. Newcastle, CA: Sierra Oaks Publishing, 1992.

INDEX

PICTURE CREDITS

MARIAN W. TAYLOR, former editor of the *New York Times* and *Los Angeles Times* syndicates, also served as an editor at *Life* magazine. Currently a New York City–based book editor and writer, she is coauthor of the *Facts on File Dictionary of New Words* and author of *Harriet Tubman* in the Chelsea House BLACK AMERICANS OF ACHIEVEMENT series.

W. DAVID BAIRD is the Howard A. White Professor of History at Pepperdine University in Malibu, California. He holds a Ph.D. from the University of Oklahoma and was formerly on the faculty of history at the University of Arkansas, Fayetteville, and Oklahoma State University. He has served as president of both the Western History Association, a professional organization, and Phi Alpha Theta, the international honor society for students of history. Dr. Baird is also the author of *The Quapaw Indians: A History of the Downstream People* and *Peter Pitchlynn: Chief of the Choctaws* and the editor of *A Creek Warrior of the Confederacy: The Autobiography of Chief G. W. Grayson.*